Women of Destiny

Women of Destiny

Planner and Prayer Journal

…The people who know their God shall be strong, and carry out *great exploits.*
Daniel 11:32

This planner belongs to

____

Date

____

Women of Destiny
Planner and Prayer Journal

Published by Penn Consulting (Publishing and Training)

 Library of Congress Cataloging in publication data
Penn, Althea
p. cm.
Women of Destiny
Summary: May this planner and journal be more than a calendar to you. It is designed to cultivate intentional spiritual growth through reflection and meditation upon God's Word. May it serve as a daily prompt to spend time in God's presence…seeking His will and purpose. May you be empowered to fulfill God's calling.
ISBN-13: 9781670656117
1. (God) Christianity –Attributes-Prayers and devotions
2. Christian women – Prayers and devotions
3. Christian women – Religious Life
4. Devotional calendars

Printed in the United States of America

The author is available for speaking events.
To find out more or book an event, please visit our websites:
www.pennconsulting.org
www.penntraining.wixsite.com/tsate
www.daughtersofsarahatl.wordpress.com/
We want to hear from you!
Please send your comments about this book to the author at apenn@pennconsulting.org.

᪥DEDICATION᪥

This book is dedicated to my Lord and Savior, Jesus Christ. Every good and perfect gift comes from above. The scriptures reveal that before the foundation of the world He was slain for my sins and yours. His sacrifice redeems us from the curse of the law and brings us into an abundant life full of meaning and purpose. The Proverbs 31 woman has many praiseworthy virtues, primarily a fear of the Lord. She is wise and resourceful. God can entrust her to employ the resources and talents she is equipped with to advance His kingdom. May this journal and the fruit of our intimate time with the Lord bring glory to the Father.

Secondly, I am eternally grateful for my family. Without the guidance and discipline of my parents, Marvin Barber and Barbara Johnson-Clark, I would probably remain lost today. By God's grace they reared me by constantly steering me towards the narrow path that leads to eternal life. Thank you for painstakingly and lovingly sharing your wisdom with me. I'm eternally grateful for my upbringing. Yet, I would be remiss if I did not mention my husband and daughters who have provided guidance and support throughout my journey to becoming a woman of destiny.

Who would have known thirty-seven years ago that the young man that walked into Westover High School's gym would be the spiritual leader, husband, and father he is today. Without his love and adoration, I surely would have given up along the way. The girls are constant sources of encouragement and joy. We rejoice as we see God's plans and purposes being fulfilled in the lives of our son-in-love and grandchildren as well. Truly we have been blessed. May the Lord continually perfect all that concerns you (Psalm 138:8).

He has made everything beautiful in its time: also he has put eternity in men's hearts, so that no man can find out the work that God does from the beginning to the end. Ecclesiastes 3:11

About the author

Dr. Penn is a licensed minister of the gospel of Jesus Christ and one of the founding members of a covenant women's group that meets regularly to cultivate spiritual growth and accountability. She has a passion for seeing educators develop in their knowledge of the one who created them and their relationships with others. She promotes spiritual formation and faith development through facilitating discipleship small group meetings and Bible studies. Her goal is to help each woman to overcome barriers to the discovery of her life's purpose and fulfillment of her Divine destiny. She has over thirty years of experience in ministry serving as a Women's and Children's Ministry leader, Bible teacher, PreK-12 teacher, and Christian school principal. She has earned degrees in Christian education administration and organization development and is a nationally certified educational administrator and professional development specialist. Her search for the meaning of it all, family crises, and multiple professional blunders equips her to humbly share with women of faith. She is a featured conference speaker and an educational consultant who has trained thousands of board members, owners, and program directors of preschools and private schools. She is married to her best friend and high school sweetheart. They have two beautiful daughters, a handsome son-in-love, and three grandchildren. They are the founders of The Shepherd's Academy for Teaching Excellence in Atlanta, GA.

This is the LORD'S doing; it is marvelous in our eyes. Psalm 118:23

Connect online at:
apennconsulting@gmail.com
www.pennconsulting.org
http://twitter.com/pennconsulting
http://linkedin.com/althea-penn
www.facebook.com/groups/childcaredirectorsroundtable
www.facebook.com/groups/purposedrivenearlyeducators

Other resources are available at: http://www.amazon.com/Althea-F.-Penn/

Other titles by the author
A Very Present Help: A 30 Day Devotional for Women of Faith
Ambassadors: Public Speaking for Children
Bullies Don't Bother Me: Biblical Conflict Resolution Strategies for Children
Classroom Management Strategy Toolbox and Planner: Proactive and Practical Classroom Management Strategies
Disorder Fact Sheet: For Parents and Teachers of Exceptional Learners
Effective Planning and Administration of Programs for Young Children
Equipping and Empowering Early Educators
Firmly Rooted: Cultivating Faith Development in the Next Generation
He is…A Planner and Journal for Christian Early Educators
The Christian Education Mandate: Equipping Kingdom Educators and Children to Impact the World for Christ
Early Education Program Administration Toolkit: Intentionally Building Capacity in Individuals and Early Childhood Organizations

Table of Contents

All scripture is inspired by God and profitable for teaching, for reproof, for correction, for training in righteousness, so that the man of God may be adequate, equipped for every good work. (2 Timothy 3:16-17)

☙ ACKNOWLEDGMENTS ❧

This prayer journal and planner is dedicated to the Daughters of Sarah, a covenant group of women who met and worshipped together in a local Baptist congregation during the early nineties. These women individually and collectively discovered their identities and purposes in Christ. They began to meet from house-to-house for times of prayer, bible study, and fellowship in 1993. They were compelled by God's love to disciple younger women who were navigating the numerous minefields that ensnare women as they grow in Christ likeness and enter ministry. They were challenged by the exhortation to faith, holiness, and submission that is found in 1 Peter 3:

"Wives, likewise, *be* submissive to your own husbands, that even if some do not obey the word, they, without a word, may be won by the conduct of their wives, when they observe your *chaste conduct accompanied* by fear. Do not let your adornment be *merely* outward—arranging the hair, wearing gold, or putting on *fine* apparel—rather *let it be* the hidden person of the heart, with the incorruptible *beauty* of a gentle and quiet spirit, which is very precious in the sight of God. For in this manner, in former times, the *holy women who trusted in God* also adorned themselves, being submissive to their own husbands, as Sarah obeyed Abraham, calling him lord, whose daughters you are if you do good and are not afraid with any terror" (1 Peter 3:1-6

They are committed to promoting the spiritual growth of others by:
☙ Equipping women in their knowledge of God, understanding of the Scripture, and their relationship with Christ and others.
☙ Enabling women to apply the Word of God to every area of their lives.
☙ Encouraging women to serve in the body of Christ and in their communities with excellence.
☙ Edifying women so they can share the love of Christ with our community and ultimately the world.

"We proclaim Him … that we may present everyone mature in Jesus Christ." Colossians 1:28

Over the past 26 years, the Daughters of Sarah have been scattered throughout the southeast United States by family and ministry transitions, yet we continue to meet annually for a prayer breakfast. Each of the women exemplify the attributes of the Proverbs 31 woman. They are women of faith, who strive to be godly wives and mothers by serving the needs of their families and communities. They are faithful stewards of the resources entrusted to them (e.g. time, treasure, temple, talents, and the like). These Titus 2 women are industrious in the workplace and in ministry.

The core Daughters of Sarah members are: Patricia Goldsby, who has demonstrated faithfulness in 50 years of marriage and ministry to her family. She and her husband John are consummate gardeners and entrepreneurs. Annie McFadden exudes wisdom in parenting as well as her consecrated lifestyle as a widow. She demonstrated remarkable faith in leaving corporate America to pursue a Biblical counseling ministry. Derona King serves as the Executive Director of Citizen's Advocacy of Atlanta and Dekalb and not only serves as an advocate for people with developmental disabilities but has served in women's ministry and wellness for more than three decades. I've learned volumes about the mysteries of marriage from her and Carl. Belinda Ringo, the only veteran in the group, introduced us all to inductive bible study methods and spiritual warfare. She and her husband Carl are hospitable hosts. Last but not least, is Laura Wilson, who radiates the compassion, grace, and truth of Christ in her evangelistic endeavors. She and Clint are always just a phone call away.

We've been blessed to have many other women join us for the annual prayer gathering consistently over the years. We appreciate the contributions made by these king makers: Lisa Baptiste, LaChrisa Bonds, Lorraine Brown, Barbara Clark, Doris Cole, Renae Cuffie, Wendy Gates, Sepia Gladden, Tonya Groomes, Lolita Whitenburg-Martin, Winfred Mbogo- Nasieku, Alynthia Penn, Charlette Pines, Arlene Robie, Diane Robinson, the late Betty Shipley, Deborah Thomas, and Deborah White. Many others have shared their gifts and talents with us as we gather to seek God's guidance and give thanks for His faithfulness.

The wisdom gleaned from sitting at the feet of Jesus with these women is weaved through every book, workshop, and interaction. Our unique callings, personalities, and stations in life reflect the tapestry found within the kingdom of God. As we speak the truth in love, we provoke women of all ages to grow in grace and a knowledge of our Lord and Savior Jesus Christ. We've joyfully encouraged one another, raised children, and are now watching our grandchildren as they begin their journeys of faith.

May our testimony remind you, that you are not alone in your quest to know Christ and make Him known. God wants you to fulfill the purpose for which you were created as much as you'd like to. Covenant relationships with holy women of God can make the journey so much lighter and make navigating challenging periods easier. It is my prayer that every woman who uses this journal and planner will enjoy relationships within the body of Christ that strengthen your faith, sharpen your gifts, and produce fruit for His glory.

For this is the way the holy women of the past who put their hope in God used to adorn themselves. They submitted themselves to their own husbands, like Sarah, who obeyed Abraham and called him her lord. You are her daughters if you do what is right and do not give way to fear. 1 Peter 3:5-6

☙ PREFACE ❧

Women of destiny know they are created for more. We feel awkward in this world because we realize this world is not our home. We understand that we are ambassadors and ministers of reconciliation, called as watchmen for such a time as this. In the midst of tragedy, natural disasters, economic turmoil, social injustices, and political crisis we think and sound differently from carnal women. The reason why is because we are in the secret place receiving marching orders from heaven. We are each designed and destined to accomplish some task in the 21st century. The apostle Paul reminds us that we are *"His workmanship, created in Christ Jesus for good works, which God prepared beforehand that we should walk in them"* (Ephesians 2:10). In order to complete our predestined assignment, we must intentionally seek God every day, hour, and minute. We are to cast all of our cares upon Him. He has given us His Word as an anchor for our souls, a light to our feet, and literally a light to our path. We cannot allow the cares of this world to deter or diminish God's purposes in our lives.

The times we live in are very much like the times that Daniel served in Babylon. God's people have fallen into idolatrous practices, are prideful, and many have been taken captive by the systems of this world. God's judgments are seen throughout the earth. During the Babylonian captivity God raised up Daniel to be His messenger. His name means "God is judge." We understand that "*the LORD is our judge,…our lawgiver, and…our king; he will save us (Isaiah 33:22).* Repeatedly we are reminded of this in the scripture: *The LORD has established His throne in the heavens; And His sovereignty rules over all (Psalm 103:19). But our God is in the heavens; He does whatever He pleases (Psalm 115:3). For I know that the LORD is great, And that our Lord is above all gods. Whatever the LORD pleases, He does, In heaven and in earth, in the seas and in all deeps (Psalm 135:5-6).* God, as the Most High God and sovereign LORD of the Universe reigns and rules over the forces of nature, seemingly random events, the daily affairs of our lives, even life, death, suffering, and pregnancy. No one can thwart God's plans. A revelation of His attributes is significant as we prepare for the second coming of the Messiah.

Our weekly prayer and Bible study enables us to cultivate a Biblical worldview. We meditated upon the book of Isaiah in 2017. It was a timely study that was very relevant to the prayer issues of the times in which we live. We observed how God's chosen people and all the inhabitants of the earth had transgressed His laws, changed the ordinances they received from Him, and broken the everlasting covenant. Isaiah prophesied from 739–681 B.C. to a divided kingdom who had turned a deaf ear to Him. Instead of serving Him with humility and offering love to their neighbors; Judah offered meaningless sacrifices in God's temple at Jerusalem and committed injustices throughout the nation; while Ephraim (the northern kingdom) rejected God, neglected His word, and were disobedient to God's commands. They turned their backs on God and alienated themselves from Him, which led to Isaiah's pronouncements of judgment. Although they responded in pride, defiance, and were incorrigible; God promised a Messiah would come to save them and us, in the hope that God's chosen people would return to Him. He reveals secrets and what will come to pass (His-story of redemption) to those who have an ear to hear. We found there is judgment during these end times but hope for believers who live the Word and have a sense of urgency in fulfilling the Great Commission. *For thus saith the LORD God, the Holy One of Israel; In returning and rest shall you be saved; in quietness and in confidence shall be your strength: and you would not.* (Isiah 30:15) We were challenged to repent and serve from a position of abiding in the LORD, drawing from His strength so that the world might know His restoring power. "I am the LORD your Savior, and your Redeemer, the Mighty One of Jacob." (Isaiah 49:26)

In 2018, we prayed through the book of Daniel. It was comforting to learn of the prophecies of the soon coming King. The Messiah will soon return for a bride without spot or wrinkle. Bible scholars describe the Book of Daniel as “a companion to the Book of Revelation” because it reveals “the sovereignty of God over the affairs of men in all ages.” It covers the activities of a covenant keeping God on behalf of His people, for the expression of His glory.

Although our citizenship is in heaven, we have been instructed to occupy this fallen world until Jesus’ return. The Book of Daniel challenged us to walk more faithfully with God as we see His inclusive plan for us during the last days. Three common themes throughout each chapter were: 1) God is the ruler, KING of all kings, and LORD of all lords; 2) He is a righteous judge, and 3) we are His ambassadors. Like Daniel, we glorify the Father when we 1) choose purity in all aspects of life; 2) we demonstrate faith and integrity in every circumstance; 3) we honor leaders (good or bad); 4) we are prayerful in the midst of trials; 5) we humble ourselves and gain supernatural insight (e.g. handwriting on the wall and vision interpretation); 6) maintain an eternal perspective of God’s sovereign rule over earthly rulers; and 7) we believe and receive the fulfillment of the promises of God.

We began 2019 with a study of the book of Colossians. The message of this epistle is greatly needed today. Numerous voices are telling us the Bible is irrelevant and we need more than Jesus Christ in order to experience true freedom—some exciting experience, some deeper doctrine, some addition to our Christian faith. But Paul affirms that what I need is to apply the truth of scripture. ‘And ye are complete in Him.’ We are warned: ‘Let no man beguile you, let no man spoil you, let no man judge you.’ The fullness of Christ is all that you need, and all man-made regulations and disciplines cannot replace the riches you have in Jesus.

“Paul was at that time a prisoner in Rome (Acts 21:17 – 28:31). He met a runaway slave named Onesimus, who belonged to Philemon, one of the leaders of the church in Colossae. Paul led Onesimus to Christ. He then wrote to Philemon, asking his friend to forgive Onesimus and receive him back as a brother in Christ. About the same time, Epaphras came to Rome because he needed Paul’s help. Some new doctrines were being taught in Colossae and were invading the church and creating problems. Paul wrote to the Colossians in order to refute these heretical teachings and establish the truth of the Gospel.” We are barraged with deceptive and dangerous heresy today! When we make Jesus Christ and the Christian revelation only part of a total religious system or philosophy, we cease to give Him the preeminence. Christian believers must beware of syncretism (mixing their Christian faith with such alluring things as yoga, transcendental meditation, oriental mysticism, and the like). We must also beware of ‘deeper life’ teachers who offer a system for victory and fullness that bypasses devotion to Jesus Chris and obedience to the Word. In all things, He must have the preeminence!”

We ended 2019 in the book of Ezekiel. The book begins with the prophet Ezekiel seeing visions of God’s glory while in exile. Like Ezekiel, we are to be watchmen on the wall; warning the wicked to repent and the righteous to stand firm in the truth of God’s Word. We are to embrace the anointing to prepare nations for the Messiah’s return. We are to repent of syncretism and be the faithful bride of Christ. He wants to present us to Himself holy and blameless. As we prayerfully begin each day and abide in Him throughout each day, God renews our minds. We are challenged to develop a Biblical worldview and defend the faith. This can only occur as we diligently seek Him and study His Word. May you behold wondrous things from His Word throughout this year!

...seek the peace of the city where I have caused you to be carried away captive, and pray to the LORD for it; for in its peace you will have peace. Jeremiah 29:7

Year-At-A-Glance Calendars

2020 Year-At-A-Glance

Therefore we must give the more earnest heed to the things we have heard,
lest we drift away. Hebrews 2:1

Month	Sun	Mon	Tue	Wed	Thu	Fri	Sat
Dec 2019	**29** Week No 52	**30**	**31**	**1** New Year's Day	**2**	**3**	**4**
Jan 2020	**5** Week No 1	**6**	**7**	**8**	**9**	**10**	**11**
	12 Week No 2	**13**	**14**	**15**	**16**	**17**	**18**
	19 Week No 3	**20** Martin Luther King Jr.'s Day	**21**	**22**	**23**	**24**	**25**
	26 Week No 4	**27**	**28**	**29**	**30**	**31**	**1**
Feb 2020	**2** Week No 5	**3**	**4**	**5**	**6**	**7**	**8**
	9 Week No 6	**10**	**11**	**12** Lincoln's Birthday	**13**	**14**	**15**
	16 Week No 7	**17** President's Day	**18**	**19**	**20**	**21**	**22**
	23 Week No 8	**24**	**25**	**26**	**27**	**28**	**29**
Mar 2020	**1** Week No 9	**2**	**3**	**4**	**5**	**6**	**7**
	8 Week No 10	**9**	**10**	**11**	**12**	**13**	**14**
	15 Week No 11	**16**	**17** St. Patrick's Day	**18**	**19**	**20**	**21**
	22 Week No 12	**23**	**24**	**25**	**26**	**27**	**28**
	29 Week No 13	**30**	**31**	**1**	**2**	**3**	**4**

Month	Sun	Mon	Tue	Wed	Thu	Fri	Sat
Apr 2020	5 Week No 14 Palm Sunday	6	7	8	9	10 Good Friday	11
	12 Week No 15 Easter	13	14	15	16	17	18
	19 Week No 16	20	21	22	23	24	25
	26 Week No 17	27	28	29	30	1	2
May 2020	3 Week No 18	4	5	6	7	8	9
	10 Week No 19 Mother's Day	11	12	13	14	15	16
	17 Week No 20	18	19	20	21	22	23
	24 Week No 21	25 Memorial Day	26	27	28	29	30
	31 Week No 22	1	2	3	4	5	6
Jun 2020	7 Week No 23	8	9	10	11	12	13
	14 Week No 24	15	16	17	18	19	20
	21 Week No 25 Father's Day	22	23	24	25	26	27
	28 Week No 26	29	30	1	2	3	4 Independence Day
Jul 2020	5 Week No 27	6	7	8	9	10	11
	12 Week No 28	13	14	15	16	17	18
	19 Week No 29	20	21	22	23	24	25

Month	Sun	Mon	Tue	Wed	Thu	Fri	Sat
	26 Week No 30	**27**	**28**	**29**	**30**	**31**	**1**
Aug 2020	**2** Week No 31	**3**	**4**	**5**	**6**	**7**	**8**
	9 Week No 32	**10**	**11**	**12**	**13**	**14**	**15**
	16 Week No 33	**17**	**18**	**19**	**20**	**21**	**22**
	23 Week No 34	**24**	**25**	**26**	**27**	**28**	**29**
	30 Week No 35	**31**	**1**	**2**	**3**	**4**	**5**
Sep 2020	**6** Week No 36	**7** Labor Day	**8**	**9**	**10**	**11**	**12**
	13 Week No 37	**14**	**15**	**16**	**17**	**18**	**19**
	20 Week No 38	**21**	**22**	**23**	**24**	**25**	**26**
	27 Week No 39	**28**	**29**	**30**	**1**	**2**	**3**
Oct 2020	**4** Week No 40	**5**	**6**	**7**	**8**	**9**	**10**
	11 Week No 41	**12** Columbus Day	**13**	**14**	**15**	**16**	**17**
	18 Week No 42	**19**	**20**	**21**	**22**	**23**	**24**
	25 Week No 43	**26**	**27**	**28**	**29**	**30**	**31**
Nov 2020	**1** Week No 44	**2**	**3**	**4**	**5**	**6**	**7**
	8 Week No 45	**9**	**10**	**11**	**12**	**13**	**14**

Month	Sun	Mon	Tue	Wed	Thu	Fri	Sat
	15 Week No 46	**16**	**17**	**18**	**19**	**20**	**21**
	22 Week No 47	**23**	**24**	**25**	**26** Thanksgiving Day	**27**	**28**
	29 Week No 48	**30**	**1**	**2**	**3**	**4**	**5**
	6 Week No 49	**7**	**8**	**9**	**10**	**11** Hanukkah	**12**
	13 Week No 50	**14**	**15**	**16**	**17**	**18**	**19**
Dec 2020	**20** Week No 51	**21**	**22**	**23**	**24**	**25** Christmas	**26**
	27 Week No 52	**28**	**29**	**30**	**31**	**1** New Year's Day	**2**

2021 Year-At-A-Glance

This *is* the day the LORD has made; We will rejoice and be glad in it. Psalm 118:24

JANUARY

S	M	T	W	T	F	S
					1	2
3	4	5	6	7	8	9
10	11	12	13	14	15	16
17	18	19	20	21	22	23
24	25	26	27	28	29	30
31						

FEBRUARY

S	M	T	W	T	F	S
	1	2	3	4	5	6
7	8	9	10	11	12	13
14	15	16	17	18	19	20
21	22	23	24	25	26	27
28						

MARCH

S	M	T	W	T	F	S
	1	2	3	4	5	6
7	8	9	10	11	12	13
14	15	16	17	18	19	20
21	22	23	24	25	26	27
28	29	30	31			

APRIL

S	M	T	W	T	F	S
				1	2	3
4	5	6	7	8	9	10
11	12	13	14	15	16	17
18	19	20	21	22	23	24
25	26	27	28	29	30	

MAY

S	M	T	W	T	F	S
						1
2	3	4	5	6	7	8
9	10	11	12	13	14	15
16	17	18	19	20	21	22
23	24	25	26	27	28	29
30	31					

JUNE

S	M	T	W	T	F	S
		1	2	3	4	5
6	7	8	9	10	11	12
13	14	15	16	17	18	19
20	21	22	23	24	25	26
27	28	29	30			

JULY

S	M	T	W	T	F	S
				1	2	3
4	5	6	7	8	9	10
11	12	13	14	15	16	17
18	19	20	21	22	23	24
25	26	27	28	29	30	31

AUGUST

S	M	T	W	T	F	S
1	2	3	4	5	6	7
8	9	10	11	12	13	14
15	16	17	18	19	20	21
22	23	24	25	26	27	28
29	30	31				

SEPTEMBER

S	M	T	W	T	F	S
			1	2	3	4
5	6	7	8	9	10	11
12	13	14	15	16	17	18
19	20	21	22	23	24	25
26	27	28	29	30		

OCTOBER

S	M	T	W	T	F	S
					1	2
3	4	5	6	7	8	9
10	11	12	13	14	15	16
17	18	19	20	21	22	23
24	25	26	27	28	29	30
31						

NOVEMBER

S	M	T	W	T	F	S
	1	2	3	4	5	6
7	8	9	10	11	12	13
14	15	16	17	18	19	20
21	22	23	24	25	26	27
28	29	30				

DECEMBER

S	M	T	W	T	F	S
			1	2	3	4
5	6	7	8	9	10	11
12	13	14	15	16	17	18
19	20	21	22	23	24	25
26	27	28	29	30	31	

1 Jan. New Year's Day
18 Jan. Birthday of Martin Luther King, Jr.
15 Feb. Washington's Birthday (Presidents' Day)
4 Apr. Easter
31 May Memorial Day
4 July Independence Day
6 Sept. Labor Day
11 Oct. Columbus Day
11 Nov. Veterans Day
25 Nov. Thanksgiving Day
25 Dec. Christmas

ꕥ2021 Holy Land -Israel
Roots of our Faith Tourꕥ

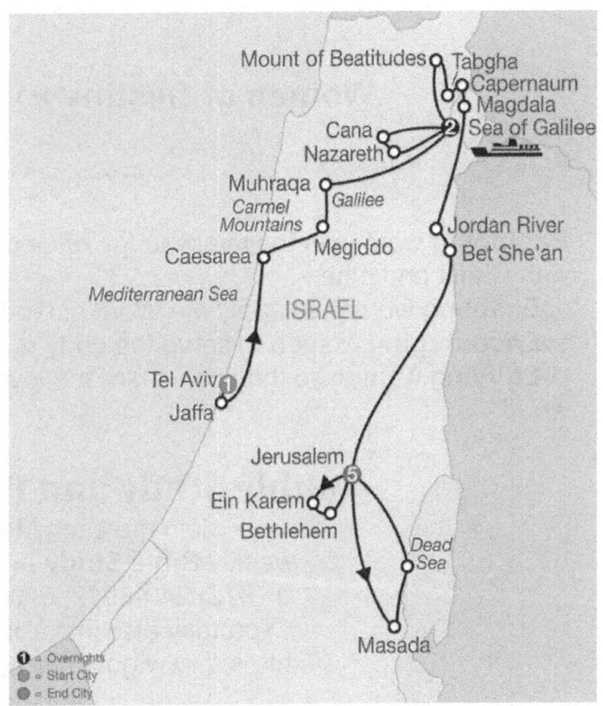

Mark your calendar and join us for the Israel Roots of our Faith Tour March 6-15, 2021

We will:

- Visit the Mount of Beatitudes where Jesus preached the Sermon on the Mount.
- Stand on the Mount of Olives in Jerusalem and reflect on the Lord's ascension into heaven.
- Take time for reflection at the Church of the Holy Sepulcher, float in the Dead Sea, and be baptized in the Jordan River.
- Walk through the historic Christian & Jewish quarters of the Old City. Take a break and shop at the bazaars.
- Visit Mt. Zion, where the Tomb of King David and the Upper Room of the Last Supper are located and so much more…

Register online or obtain additional information at http://www.americaisraeltours.com/christian-tours-israel/roots-of-your-faith/#itinerary

Join our Facebook group in order to stay abreast of trip plans and progress: https://www.facebook.com/groups/IsraelTour2021/

March 20, 2020 $250 deposit due (We qualify for a $75 discount if 10 people are registered)

April 20-January 20, 2020 $200/month

Wire transfers may be made via Zelle® by sending payments to Dr. Penn at (678) 557-8684 or you may send payments directly to America Israel Tours.

- Tentative travel dates: March 6 – 15, 2021 (10 days/7 nights)
- $2,260 per person dual occupancy room covers the licensed professional tour, lodging, tour guide, transfers, hotels, breakfast & dinner, attraction/site fees and lifetime memories!
- $3,185 per person private room
- Other tour costs include: $600-1,800 for the airline ticket-purchase on your own
- Gratuities: $75 (per person)
- One day early arrival includes: airport transfer, dinner/breakfast and hotel night stay: $220 (pp based on dual occupancy)
- ***3% DISOCUNT FOR CHECK PAYMENTS.***
- $250 per person deposit required to secure tour. Final payment due 60 days prior to travel.
- Parties of 6 – 9 receive a $50 pp discount. Parties of 10 – 15 receive a $75 pp discount. Parties of 18+ require private tour pricing.
- **Like us on Facebook! - https://www.facebook.com/pg/AmericaIsraelTours/reviews/**
- Click here for information detailing our **Hotels - https://www.americaisraeltours.com/christian-tours-israel/roots-of-your-faith/#hotels**
- Click here for information detailing our **Travel Insurance - http://www.americaisraeltours.com/travel-insurance/**
- Click here for information detailing our **Terms & Conditions - http://www.americaisraeltours.com/terms-conditions/**

Women of Destiny ꟾ Covenant Women of Faith

"We proclaim Him … that we may present everyone mature in Jesus Christ." Colossians 1:28

Equipping women in their knowledge of God, understanding of the Scripture, and relationship with Christ and others.
ꟾ**Enabling** women to apply the Word of God to every area of their lives.
ꟾ**Encouraging** women to serve the body of Christ and in the community with excellence.
ꟾ**Edifying** women so they can share the love of Christ with our community and ultimately the world.

ꟾBible Study and Prayer Teleconferenceꟾ

Join me each Monday 12-1 p.m. for the
weekly **Bible Study and Prayer Teleconference** at
1 (872) 240-3212, enter access code 279-599-357.
You may also join from your computer or tablet at
https://www.gotomeet.me/DaughtersofSarahprayer.

… do not cease to give thanks for you, making mention of you in my prayers: that the God of our Lord Jesus Christ, the Father of glory, may give to you the spirit of wisdom and revelation in the knowledge of Him, the eyes of your understanding being enlightened; that you may know what is the hope of His calling, what are the riches of the glory of His inheritance in the saints, and what *is* the exceeding greatness of His power toward us who believe,…
Ephesians 1:16-19a

ᏇSpiritual Growth GoalsᏇ

…seek first the kingdom of God and His righteousness… Matthew 6:33a

I press on toward the goal for the prize of the upward call of God in Christ Jesus. Philippians 3:14

༄ My Spiritual Growth Plan ༄

Spiritual growth is the intentional process of increasing in Christ likeness by aligning our will with the purpose of God for our lives. It should be reflected in every interaction, relationship, and area of our lives. Prayerfully set realistic goals using the scriptures below as a guide. As you fix your focus and efforts, it will enable you to experience optimal growth. There are no limits to what is possible with God! As the apostle Paul prayed, may God "grant you, according to the riches of His glory, to be strengthened with might through His Spirit in the inner man, that Christ may dwell in your hearts through faith; that you, being rooted and grounded in love, may be able to comprehend with all the saints what *is* the width and length and depth and height—to know the love of Christ which passes knowledge; that you may be filled with all the fullness of God." (Ephesians 3:16-19)

Spiritual - That we henceforth *be no more children* ... but speaking the truth in love, may *grow up* into Him in all things ...Ephesians 4:14, 15
Devotional - Daily Time, Journaling, Bible Study (Proverbs 8:17)
Church Involvement/Community Service (Ephesians 2:10)
Application of Spiritual Gifts (Romans 12, 1 Corinthians 12)
Relational - By this shall all men know that ye are my disciples, if ye have love one to another. John 13:35
Spouse (Ephesians 5:21-25)
Parents (Ephesians 6:4)
Children (Exodus 20:12)
Siblings, Friends (Proverbs 17:17,13:20)

Physical – Therefore, I urge you brothers, in view of God's mercy, to offer your bodies as living sacrifices, holy and pleasing to God-this is your spiritual act of worship. Romans 12:1
Exercise/Fitness (1 Corinthians 9:27, 1 Timothy 4:8)
Diet (1 Corinthians 6:19)
Sleep (Ps. 127:2)
Medical Strategy (James 5:15-16)
Appearance Needs (1 Samuel 16:7)
Mental/Emotional (Philippians 4:8, 9)
Financial - The wicked borrow and do not repay, but the righteous give generously. Psalm 37:21
Tithing (Malachi 3:8-12)
Provisions (Matthew 6:33)
Offerings (2 Corinthians 9:6-8)
Abundance (Luke 6:38)

Net Worth (Proverbs 3:9, 10)
Career-Whatever you do, work at it with all your heart, as working for the Lord, not for men, since you know that you will receive an inheritance from the Lord as a reward. It is the Lord Christ you are serving. Colossians 3:23, 24
Calling (John 15:16)
Earning (1 Timothy 5:8)
Time (Ephesians 5:15-17)

Where there is no vision, the people perish: but he that keeps the law, happy is he. Proverbs 29:18

Prayer reflections

____

____

____

____

____

____

____

____

____

____

༄Devotional Starters☙

Devote yourselves to prayer, keeping alert in it with *an attitude of* thanksgiving; praying at the same time for us as well, that God will open up to us a door for the word, so that we may speak forth the mystery of Christ…Colossians 4:2, 3a NASB

Jehovah – the self-existent, eternal, unchanging, "I am that I am," covenant-keeping God.

Jehovah is an English translation of the Hebrew name for God. The four letters יהוה (YHWH) are a Tetragrammaton. Ancient Hebrew did not use vowels in its written form. The vowels were pronounced in spoken Hebrew but were not recorded in written Hebrew. Jehovah is God's unique name as revealed in the Bible. (Exodus 3:15; Psalm 83:18) It describes His role as the Creator and the Fulfiller of his purposes. (Isaiah 55:10, 11) The Bible reveals the Person behind the name Jehovah, especially His dominant quality of love.—Exodus 34:5-7; Luke 6:35; 1 John 4:8. He created you for relationship and fellowship with Him.

Knowing God, His nature, His character, His purposes, and plans will radically transform your life. There are countless benefits to knowing who He is and infinite advantages to knowing who you are, especially in Christ. Your very existence is based upon the Father God's eternal purposes (Psalm 91, Romans 8:28-31, Ephesians 2:10). Why not journal the things he reveals as you use this daily planner and journal? By the end of the year I am sure you will have experienced transformation, growth, deliverance, and breakthrough in every area of your life. May He grant you the desires of your heart and fulfill His purposes. Psalm 20:4

He is... *I am...*

- Jehovah Nissi (The Lord my banner) Ex. 17:15

___

- Jehovah-Raah (Roi) (The Lord my shepherd) Ps. 23

___

- Jehovah Rapha (The Lord my healer) Ex. 15:26

___

- Jehovah Shammah (The Lord is here) Ez. 48:35

___

- Jehovah Tsidkenu (The Lord our righteousness) Jer. 23:6

___

- Jehovah Mekoddishkem (The Lord who sanctifies me) Ex. 31:13

___

- Jehovah Jireh (The Lord my provider) Ge. 22:14

___

ꕥ Jehovah Shalom (The Lord my peace) Jg. 6:24

___

ꕥ Jehovah Sabaoth (The Lord of hosts) Ps. 24:10

___

ꕥ *He is...* – The counsel of the LORD stands forever, The plans of His heart to all generations. Psalm 33:11

A. Omniscient (all-knowing): ___

B. Omnipresent (all pervading): ___

C. Omnipotent (all-powerful, almighty): ___

ꕥ *I am...* – For by grace you have been saved through faith; and that not of yourselves, *it is* the gift of God; not as a result of works, so that no one may boast. For we are His workmanship, created in Christ Jesus for good works, which God prepared beforehand so that we would walk in them. Ephesians 2:8-10

A. Saved: ___

B. Significant: ___

C. Sent: ___

ꕥ *I have...* – Go therefore and make disciples of all the nations, baptizing them in the name of the Father and of the Son and of the Holy Spirit, teaching them to observe all things that I have commanded you; and lo, I am with you always, *even* to the end of the age." Amen. Matthew 28:19-20

A. Purpose: ___

B. Provision: ___

C. Power: ___

...Many more believed because of His own words. Then they said to the woman, "Now we believe, not because of what you said, for we ourselves have heard *Him* and we know that this is indeed the Christ, the Savior of the world." John 4:41, 42

Because He is...

___

___

___

≀Bible Reading Plan∽

Be doers of the word, and not hearers only.
Otherwise, you are deceiving yourselves. James 1:22

Why read through the Bible in a year?

Many Christians evaluate their Bible reading habits, and then change or begin a Bible reading plan at the beginning of the year. You can really begin any time of the year. It is a good idea to note aspects of God's character as they are revealed in each book of the Bible. Ultimately, above the 40 human authors who wrote over a 1,500 year period, from three different continents, the Bible was written by God. 2 Timothy 3:16 tells us that the Bible was "breathed out or inspired" by God. God superintended the human authors of the Bible so that, while using their God-given writing styles, perceptions, and personalities, they recorded exactly what God intended. The Bible was not dictated by God, but it was perfectly guided and entirely inspired by Him.

There are 66 books in the Bible with 1,189 chapters made up of 31,173 verses and we find perfect harmony in the message they convey. The Bible introduces us to Jesus Christ and reveals that "whatever things were written aforetime were written for our learning, that we through patience and comfort of the scriptures might have hope." (Romans 15:4) You will strengthen your faith and discover your identity. A second purpose for the scripture is that we might grow and be "thoroughly furnished" for the good works for which we were created (Ephesians 2:10, 2 Timothy 2:17b).

Below is a suggested reading plan and chart to record your observations of who God is in each book of the Bible. May the Word of God be a lamp to your feet and a light to your path. (Psalm 119:105) Hearing and obeying the word of God will prevent your deception and strengthen your foundation. Jesus said, "Therefore whoever hears these sayings of mine, and does them, I will liken him to a wise man, which built his house on a rock." (Matthew 7:24) He is that firm foundation and wants you firmly rooted.

If you live in the part of the United States known as *Tornado Alley*, where tornados are most frequent, you are aware of what happens when a big storm hits. Strong winds whip through and trees that have shallow roots are uprooted and tossed about like toothpicks. But trees with deep roots that go far into the ground are anchored in place. These deeply rooted trees continue to grow year after year and survive storm after storm. In the same way, God challenges us to stand firm, have those same kinds of deep roots.

Father,

Help me to desire and enjoy reading your Word. The writer of Hebrews exclaims that its impossible to please you without faith and that faith comes by hearing. Help me to diligently spend time with you each day. Bless my efforts to read and understand Your Word. Open my mind and heart to what you would have me to learn from Your Word. Give me the strength to be obedient to Your Word. Plant within me the growing desire to learn Your Word. Let me be led by your Word. May it bring forth fruit in every area of my life. In Jesus' name. Amen

READ THROUGH THE BIBLE IN ONE YEAR

JANUARY		25	34-36	18	6-7	9	11-15	2	57-59
GENESIS		*DEUTERONOMY*		19	8	10	16-21	3	60-63
1	1-3	26	1-2	20	9-11	11	22-27	4	64-66
2	4-7	27	3-4	21	12-13	12	28-31	*JEREMIAH*	
3	8-10	28	5-6	22	14-16	13	32-36	5	1-3
4	11-14	MARCH		23	17-18	14	37-40	6	4-5
5	15-18	1	7-9	24	19-20	15	41 &	7	6-7
6	19-21	2	10-12	25	21-22	*PSALMS*		8	8-10
7	22-24	3	13-15	*2 KINGS*		15	1-5	9	11-13
8	25-26	4	16-19	26	1-3	16	6-16	10	14-16
9	27-29	5	20-22	27	4-5	17	17-21	11	17-19
10	30-31	6	23-26	28	6-8	18	22-29	12	20-22
11	32-34	7	27-28	29	9-10	19	30-35	13	23-25
12	35-37	8	29-31	30	11-13	20	36-41	14	26-28
13	38-40	9	32-34	MAY		21	42-49	15	29-30
14	41-42	*JOSHUA*		1	14-16	22	50-57	16	31-32
15	43-44	10	1-3	2	17-18	23	58-66	17	33-35
16	45-47	11	4-6	3	19-21	24	67-71	18	36-38
17	48-50	12	7-8	4	22-23	25	72-77	19	39-42
EXODUS		13	9-10	5	24-25	26	78-81	20	43-46
18	1-3	14	11-14	*1 CHRONICLES*		27	82-89	21	47-49
19	4-6	15	15-17	6	1-3	28	90-98	22	50
20	7-8	16	18-20	7	4-5	29	99-104	23	51-52
21	9-11	17	21-22	8	6-7	30	105-108	*LAMENTATIONS*	
22	12-13	18	23-24	9	8-10	JULY		24	1-2
23	14-16	*JUDGES*		10	11-13	1	109-118	25	3-5
24	17-19	19	1-3	11	14-16	2	119	*EZEKIEL*	
25	20-22	20	4-6	12	17-20	3	120-135	26	1-4
26	23-25	21	7-8	13	21-23	4	136-143	27	5-7
27	26-28	22	9-10	14	24-26	5	144-150	28	8-11
28	29-30	23	11-13	15	27-29	*PROVERBS*		29	12-14
29	31-33	24	14-16	*2 CHRONICLES*		6	1-5	30	15-16
30	34-35	25	17-19	16	1-4	7	6-9	31	17-19
31	36-38	26	20-21	17	5-7	8	10-13	SEPTEMBER	
FEBRUARY		*RUTH*		18	8-11	9	14-17	1	20-21
1	39-40	27	1-4	19	12-15	10	18-21	2	22-23
LEVITICUS		*1 SAMUEL*		20	16-19	11	22-24	3	24-26
2	1-4	28	1-3	21	20-22	12	25-28	4	27-28
3	5-7	29	4-6	22	23-25	13	29-31	5	29-31
4	8-10	30	7-9	23	26-28	*ECCLESIASTES*		6	32-33
5	11-12	31	10-12	24	29-30	14	1-4	7	34-36
6	13-14	APRIL		26	31-32	15	5-8	8	37-39
7	15-17	1	13-14	27	33-34	16	9-12	9	40-42
8	18-19	2	15-16	28	35-36	*SONG/SOLOMON*		10	43-45
9	20-21	3	17-18	*EZRA*		17	1-8	11	46-48
10	23-25	4	19-21	28	1-4	*ISAIAH*		*DANIEL*	
11	26-27	5	22-24	29	5-7	18	1-4	12	1-2
NUMBERS		6	25-27	30	8-10	19	5-7	13	3-4
12	1-2	7	28-31	*NEHEMIAH*		20	8-10	14	5-6
13	3-4	*2 SAMUEL*		31	1-3	21	11-14	15	7-8
14	5-6	8	1-3	JUNE		22	15-19	16	9-10
15	7-8	9	4-7	1	4-6	23	20-24	17	11-12
16	9-11	10	8-11	2	7-8	24	25-28	*HOSEA*	
17	12-14	11	12-13	3	9-10	25	29-31	18	1-6
18	15-16	12	14-16	4	11-13	26	32-35	19	7-10
19	17-19	13	17-18	*ESTHER*		27	36-38	20	11-14
20	20-21	14	19-21	5	1-4	28	39-41	*JOEL*	
21	22-24	15	22-24	6	5-10	29	42-44	21	1-3
22	25-27	*1 KINGS*		*JOB*		30 31	45-48 49-51	*AMOS*	
23	28-30	16	1-2	7	1-5	AUGUST		22	1-5
24	31-33	17	3-5	8	6-10	1	52-56	23	6-9

READ THROUGH THE BIBLE IN ONE YEAR

OBADIAH		***MARK***		**16**	**7-8**	***2 THESSOLONIANS***	
24	**1 &**	**15**	**1-3**	**17**	**9-10**	**14**	**1-3**
JONAH		**16**	**4-5**	**18**	**11-13**	***1 TIMOTHY***	
24	**1-4**	**17**	**6-7**	**19**	**14-16**	**15**	**1-6**
MICAH		**18**	**8-9**	**20**	**17-19**	***2 TIMOTHY***	
25	**1-5**	**19**	**10-11**	**21**	**20-22**	**16**	**1-4**
26	**6-7 &**	**20**	**12-13**	**22**	**23-25**	***TITUS***	
NAHUM		**21**	**14**	**23**	**26-28**	**17**	**1 &**
26	**1-3**	**22**	**15-16**	***ROMANS***		***PHILEMON***	
HABAKKUK		***LUKE***		**24**	**1-3**	**17**	**1**
27	**1-3**	**23**	**1**	**25**	**4-7**	***HEBREWS***	
ZEPHANIAH		**24**	**2-3**	**26**	**8-10**	**18**	**1-5**
28	**1-3**	**24**	**4-5**	**27**	**11-13**	**19**	**6-10**
HAGGAI		**26**	**6-7**	**28**	**14-16**	**20**	**11-13**
29	**1-2 &**	**27**	**8**	***1 CORINTHIANS***		***JAMES***	
ZECHARIAH		**28**	**9**	**29**	**1-4**	**21**	**1-5**
29	**1-3**	**29**	**10-11**	**30**	**5-8**	***1 PETER***	
30	**4-9**	**30**	**12-13**	**DECEMBER**		**22**	**1-5**
OCTOBER		**31**	**14-16**	**1**	**9-11**	***2 PETER***	
1	**10-14**	**NOVEMBER**		**2**	**12-14**	**23**	**1-3**
MALACHI		**1**	**17-18**	**3**	**15-16**	***1 JOHN***	
2	**1-4**	**2**	**19-20**	***2 CORINTHIANS***		**24**	**1-5**
MATTHEW		**3**	**21-22**	**4**	**1-4**	***2 JOHN***	
3	**1-4**	**4**	**23-24**	**5**	**5-9**	**25**	**1 &**
4	**5-7**	***JOHN***		**6**	**10-13**	***3 JOHN***	
5	**8-10**	**5**	**1-3**	***GALATIANS***		**25**	**1 &**
6	**11-12**	**6**	**4-5**	**7**	**1-3**	***JUDE***	
7	**13-14**	**7**	**6-7**	**8**	**4-6**	**25**	**1**
8	**15-17**	**8**	**8-9**	***EPHESIANS***		***REVELATION***	
9	**18-19**	**9**	**10-11**	**9**	**1-4**	**26**	**1-3**
10	**20-21**	**10**	**12-13**	**10**	**4-6**	**27**	**4-8**
11	**22-23**	**11**	**14-16**	***PHILIPPIANS***		**28**	**9-12**
12	**24-25**	**12**	**17-18**	**11**	**1-4**	**29**	**13-16**
13	**26**	**13**	**19-21**	***COLOSSIANS***		**30**	**17-19**
14	**27-28**	***ACTS***		**12**	**1-4**	**31**	**20-22**
		14	**1-3**	***1 THESSOLONIANS***			
		15	**4-6**	**13**	**1-5**		

Jesus in every book of the Bible		
Book of the Bible	Themes(s)	Make note of how Christ is revealed in this book of the Bible
Genesis	Creation, Beginnings, Theocracy	
Exodus	Deliverance	
Leviticus	Instruction	
Numbers	Journeys	
Deuteronomy	Obedience	
Joshua	Conquest	
Judges	Deterioration Deliverance	
Ruth	Redemption	
1 Samuel	Transition	
2 Samuel	Unification	
1 Kings	Disruption	
2 Kings	Dispersion	
1 Chronicles	Israel's spiritual history	
2 Chronicles	Israel's spiritual heritage	
Ezra	Restoration	
Nehemiah	Reconstruction	
Esther	Preservation	
Job	Blessings through suffering	

Psalms	Praise	
Proverbs	Practical wisdom	
Ecclesiastes	All is vanity apart from God	
Song of Solomon	Love and marriage	
Isaiah	Salvation	
Jeremiah	Judgment	
Lamentations	Lament	
Ezekiel	The glory of the Lord	
Daniel	Sovereignty of God	
Hosea	Unfaithfulness	
Joel	The day of the Lord	
Amos	Judgment	
Obadiah	Righteous judgment	
Jonah	God's grace to all people	
Micah	Divine judgment	
Nahum	Consolation	
Habakkuk	Trusting a sovereign God	
Zephaniah	The "great day of the LORD"	
Haggai	Rebuilding the temple	

Women of Destiny

Zechariah	God's deliverance	
Malachi	Formalism rebuked	
Matthew	The kingdom of God	
Mark	The Suffering Servant	
Luke	The Perfect Man	
John	The Son of God	
Acts	The spread of the gospel	
Romans	The righteousness of God	
1 Corinthians	Christian conduct	
2 Corinthians	Paul's defense of his apostleship	
Galatians	Freedom in Christ	
Ephesians	Blessings in Christ	
Philippians	The joy-filled life	
Colossians	Supremacy of Christ	
1 Thessalonians	Concern for the church	
2 Thessalonians	Living in hope	
1 Timothy	Instructions for a young disciple	
2 Timothy	A charge to faithful ministry	

Titus	A manual of conduct	
Philemon	Forgiveness	
Hebrews	The superiority of Christ	
James	Genuine faith	
1 Peter	Responding to suffering	
2 Peter	Warning against false teachers	
1 John	Fellowship with God	
2 John	Christian discernment	
3 John	Christian hospitality	
Jude	Contending for the faith	
Revelation	The unveiling of Jesus Christ	

… without faith it is impossible to please him: for he that cometh to God must believe that he is, and that he is a rewarder of them that diligently seek him. Hebrews 11:6

꧁Monthly Calendars꧂

From the rising of the sun unto the going down of the same the LORD'S name is to be praised. Psalm 113:3

El Elyon ~ "The Most High God"

January 2020						
Sun	Mon	Tue	Wed	Thu	Fri	Sat
			1	2	3	4
5	6	7	8	9	10	11
12	13	14	15	16	17	18
19	20	21	22	23	24	25
26	27	28	29	30	31	

ᘓ Appointments & Scheduled Events ᘐ

ᘓ To Do or To Call List ᘐ

I will cry out to God Most High, to God who performs all things for me. Psalm 57:2

Elohim – “the one true God, Judge, Creator”

February 2020						
Sun	Mon	Tue	Wed	Thu	Fri	Sat
						1
2	3	4	5	6	7	8
9	10	11	12	13	14	15
16	17	18	19	20	21	22
23	24	25	26	27	28	29

ꕥ Appointments & Scheduled Events ꕥ

ꕥ To Do or To Call List ꕥ

For the LORD is our judge, the LORD is our lawgiver, the LORD is our king; he will save us.
Isaiah 33:22

Jehovah-Jireh – "the Lord my provider"

March 2020

Sun	Mon	Tue	Wed	Thu	Fri	Sat
1	2	3	4	5	6	7
8	9	10	11	12	13	14
15	16	17	18	19	20	21
22	23	24	25	26	27	28
29	30	31				

ꕤ Appointments & Scheduled Events ꕤ

ꕤ To Do or To Call List ꕤ

But my God shall supply all your need according to his riches in glory by Christ Jesus.
Philippians 4:19

Jehovah-Rophe / Raphah ~ "the Lord my healer"

April 2020						
Sun	Mon	Tue	Wed	Thu	Fri	Sat
			1	2	3	4
5	6	7	8	9	10	11
12	13	14	15	16	17	18
19	20	21	22	23	24	25
26	27	28	29	30		

༄ Appointments & Scheduled Events ༄

༄ To Do or To Call List ༄

If my people, which are called by my name, shall humble themselves, and pray, and seek my face, and turn from their wicked ways; then will I hear from heaven, and will forgive their sin, and will heal their land. 2 Chronicles 7:14

El Olam - "the Ancient of Days, the everlasting God"

May 2020

Sun	Mon	Tue	Wed	Thu	Fri	Sat
					1	2
3	4	5	6	7 National Day of Prayer	8	9
10	11	12	13	14	15	16
17	18	19	20	21	22	23
24	25	26	27	28	29	30
31						

ꕥ Appointments & Scheduled Events ꕥ

ꕥ To Do or To Call List ꕥ

Trust in the Lord forever, for in Yah, the Lord, is everlasting strength. Isaiah 26:4

Alpha and Omega ~ "the first and the last"

June 2020						
Sun	**Mon**	**Tue**	**Wed**	**Thu**	**Fri**	**Sat**
	1	**2**	**3**	**4**	**5**	**6**
7	**8**	**9**	**10**	**11**	**12**	**13**
14	**15**	**16**	**17**	**18**	**19**	**20**
21	**22**	**23**	**24**	**25**	**26**	**27**
28	**29**	**30**				

℘ Appointments & Scheduled Events ℘

℘ To Do or To Call List ℘

I am the Alpha and the Omega, the First and the Last, the Beginning and the End.
Revelation 22:13

Author and finisher - Source and Consumater

July 2020						
Sun	**Mon**	**Tue**	**Wed**	**Thu**	**Fri**	**Sat**
			1	**2**	**3**	**4**
5	**6**	**7**	**8**	**9**	**10**	**11**
12	**13**	**14**	**15**	**16**	**17**	**18**
19	**20**	**21**	**22**	**23**	**24**	**25**
26	**27**	**28**	**29**	**30**	**31**	

༄ Appointments & Scheduled Events ༄

____

____

____

____

༄ To Do or To Call List ༄

____

____

____

____

Looking unto Jesus the author and perfecter of our faith; who for the joy that was set before him endured the cross, despising the shame, and is seated at the right hand of the throne of God.
Hebrews 12:2

The Word

August 2020						
Sun	Mon	Tue	Wed	Thu	Fri	Sat
						1
2	3	4	5	6	7	8
9	10	11	12	13	14	15
16	17	18	19	20	21	22
23	24	25	26	27	28	29
30	31					

ꕥ Appointments & Scheduled Events ꕥ

ꕥ To Do or To Call List ꕥ

In the beginning was the Word, and the Word was with God, and the Word was God. John 1:1

The Way

September 2020						
Sun	Mon	Tue	Wed	Thu	Fri	Sat
		1	2	3	4	5
6	7	8	9	10	11	12
13	14	15	16	17	18	19
20	21	22	23	24	25	26
27	28	29	30			

ꕥ Appointments & Scheduled Events ꕥ

ꕥ To Do or To Call List ꕥ

Jesus said to him, I am the way, the truth, and the life: no man comes to the Father, but by me.
John 14:6

Lamb of God

October 2020

Sun	Mon	Tue	Wed	Thu	Fri	Sat
				1	2	3
4	5	6	7	8	9	10
11	12	13	14	15	16	17
18	19	20	21	22	23	24
25	26	27	28	29	30	31

ဢ Appointments & Scheduled Events ଓ

ဢ To Do or To Call List ଓ

The next day John sees Jesus coming to him, and said, Behold the Lamb of God, which takes away the sin of the world. John 1:29

Yeshua Hamashiach - Jesus the Messiah

November 2020						
Sun	Mon	Tue	Wed	Thu	Fri	Sat
1	2	3	4	5	6	7
8	9	10	11	12	13	14
15	16	17	18	19	20	21
22	23	24	25	26	27	28
29	30					

ꕥ Appointments & Scheduled Events ꕥ

ꕥ To Do or To Call List ꕥ

Now thanks be to God, which always causes us to triumph in Christ (the anointed, promised one), and makes manifest the aroma of his knowledge by us in every place. 2 Corinthians 2:14

Emmanuel ~ "God with us"

December 2020

Sun	Mon	Tue	Wed	Thu	Fri	Sat
		1	2	3	4	5
6	7	8	9	10	11	12
13	14	15	16	17	18	19
20	21	22	23	24	25	26
27	28	29	30	31		

ꟹ Appointments & Scheduled Events ꟹ

ꟹ To Do or To Call List ꟹ

…we have this treasure in earthen vessels, that the excellence of the power may be of God and not of us. 2 Corinthians 4:7

Jehovah M'kaddesh – "The Lord who sanctifies you"

January 2021

Sun	Mon	Tue	Wed	Thu	Fri	Sat
					1 New Year's Day	2
3	4	5	6	7	8	9
10	11	12	13	14	15	16
17	18 Martin Luther King Jr.	19	20 Inauguration Day	21	22	23
24	25	26	27	28	29	30
31						

ᘓ Appointments & Scheduled Events ᘐ

ᘓ To Do or To Call List ᘐ

Speak also to the children of Israel, saying: 'Surely My Sabbaths you shall keep, for it is a sign between Me and you throughout your generations, that you may know that I am the Lord who sanctifies you. Exodus 31:13

El Shaddai ~ "the Lord God Almighty"

February 2021						
	Mon	Tue	Wed	Thu	Fri	Sat
	1	2 Groundhog Day	3	4	5	6
7 Super Bowl	8	9	10	11	12	13
14 Valentine's Day	15 Presidents Day	16	17 Ash Wednesday	18	19	20
21	22	23	24	25	26	27
28						

Appointments & Scheduled Events

To Do or To Call List

May God Almighty bless you,
And make you fruitful and multiply you,
That you may be an assembly of peoples Genesis 28:3

Jehovah Nissi ~ "God is my victory banner"

March 2021						
Sun	**Mon**	**Tue**	**Wed**	**Thu**	**Fri**	**Sat**
	1	**2**	**3**	**4**	**5**	**6**
7	**8**	**9**	**10**	**11**	**12**	**13**
14 Daylight Saving Begins	**15**	**16**	**17** Saint Patrick's Day	**18**	**19**	**20** Start of Spring (Spring Equinox)
21	**22**	**23**	**24**	**25**	**26**	**27**
28	**29**	**30**	**31**			

℘ Appointments & Scheduled Events ℘

____
____
____
____
____
____
____
____

℘ To Do or To Call List ℘

____
____
____
____
____
____
____
____

Be strong and of a good courage, fear not, nor be afraid of them: for the LORD your God, he it is that does go with you; he will not fail you, nor forsake you. Deuteronomy 31:6

Jehovah-Roi ~ "the God who is my shepherd"

April 2021

Sun	Mon	Tue	Wed	Thu	Fri	Sat
				1 Holy Thursday	2 Good Friday	3
4 Easter	5	6	7	8	9	10
11	12	13	14	15 Tax Day (Taxes Due)	16	17
18	19	20	21 Administrative Professionals	22	23	24
25	26	27	28	29	30	

ꟸ Appointments & Scheduled Events ꟹ

ꟸ To Do or To Call List ꟹ

The Lord is my shepherd: I shall not want. Psalm 23:1

Jehovah-Tsidkenu – "the God who is our righteousness"

May 2021

Sun	Mon	Tue	Wed	Thu	Fri	Sat
						1
2	3	4	5	6 National Day of Prayer	7	8
9 Mother's Day	10	11	12	13	14	15 Armed Forces Day
16	17	18	19	20	21	22
23	24	25	26	27	28	29
30	31 Memorial Day					

ꕤ Appointments & Scheduled Events ꕤ

ꕤ To Do or To Call List ꕤ

It is because of Him that you are in Christ Jesus, who has become for us wisdom from God: our righteousness, holiness, and redemption. 1 Corinthians 1:30 BSB

Jehovah-Shammah ~ "the God who is omni-present"

June 2021						
Sun	**Mon**	**Tue**	**Wed**	**Thu**	**Fri**	**Sat**
		1	**2**	**3**	**4**	**5**
6	**7**	**8**	**9**	**10**	**11**	**12**
13	**14** Flag Day	**15**	**16**	**17**	**18**	**19**
20 Start of Summer (Summer Solstice)	**21**	**22**	**23**	**24**	**25**	**26**
27	**28**	**29**	**30**			

ᘛ Appointments & Scheduled Events ᘚ

ᘛ To Do or To Call List ᘚ

Let your conduct be without covetousness; and be content with such things as you have: for he has said, I will never leave you, nor forsake you. Hebrews 13:5

Jehovah-Tsaboath ~ "the God of armies"

July 2021						
Sun	**Mon**	**Tue**	**Wed**	**Thu**	**Fri**	**Sat**
				1	**2**	**3**
4 Indep. Day	**5**	**6**	**7**	**8**	**9**	**10**
11	**12**	**13**	**14**	**15**	**16**	**17**
18	**19**	**20**	**21**	**22**	**23**	**24**
25	**26**	**27**	**28**	**29**	**30**	**31**

≈ Appointments & Scheduled Events ≈

≈ To Do or To Call List ≈

For he shall give his angels charge over you, to keep you in all your ways. Psalm 91:11

Wonderful Counselor

August 2021

Sun	Mon	Tue	Wed	Thu	Fri	Sat
1	2	3	4	5	6	7
8	9	10	11	12	13	14
15	16	17	18	19	20	21
22	23	24	25	26	27	28
29	30	31				

ꕥ Appointments & Scheduled Events ꕥ

ꕥ To Do or To Call List ꕥ

For I will give you a mouth and wisdom, which all your adversaries shall not be able to contradict nor resist. Luke 21:15

The Mighty God

September 2021

Sun	Mon	Tue	Wed	Thu	Fri	Sat
			1	2	3	4
5	6 Labor Day	7	8	9	10	11 Patriot Day
12	13	14	15	16	17	18
19	20	21	22 Start of Fall (Autumnal Equinox)	23	24	25
26	27	28	29	30		

ᘓ Appointments & Scheduled Events ᘐ

ᘓ To Do or To Call List ᘐ

For with God nothing shall be impossible. Luke 1:37

Everlasting Father

October 2021						
Sun	Mon	Tue	Wed	Thu	Fri	Sat
					1	2
3	4	5	6	7	8	9
10	11 Columbus Day	12	13	14	15	16
17	18	19	20	21	22	23
24	25	26	27	28	29	30
31						

ꕥ Appointments & Scheduled Events ꕥ

ꕥ To Do or To Call List ꕥ

Now our Lord Jesus Christ himself, and God, even our Father, which has loved us, and has given us everlasting consolation and good hope through grace, comfort your hearts, and establish you in every good word and work. 2 Thessalonians 2:17

Prince of Peace

November 2021

Sun	Mon	Tue	Wed	Thu	Fri	Sat
	1	2 Election Day	3	4	5	6
7 Daylight Saving Time Ends	8	9	10	11 Veterans Day	12	13
14	15	16	17	18	19	20
21	22	23	24	25 Thanksgiving Day	26	27
28	29	30				

೫ Appointments & Scheduled Events ೪

೫ To Do or To Call List ೪

Be careful for nothing; but in everything by prayer and supplication with thanksgiving let your requests be made known to God. And the peace of God, which passes all understanding, shall keep your hearts and minds through Christ Jesus. Philippians 4:6, 7

Jesus ~ "Savior and Redeemer"

December 2021

Sun	Mon	Tue	Wed	Thu	Fri	Sat
			1	2	3	4
5	6	7	8	9	10	11
12	13	14	15	16	17	18
19	20	21 Start of Winter (Winter Solstice)	22	23	24	25 Christmas
26	27	28	29	30	31	

ꕤ Appointments & Scheduled Events ꕤ

ꕤ To Do or To Call List ꕤ

Who has delivered us from the power of darkness, and has translated us into the kingdom of his dear Son: In whom we have redemption through his blood, even the forgiveness of sins...Colossians 1:13, 14

ꕤ *Journaling* ꕤ

...Write all the words that I have spoken unto you in a book.
Jeremiah 30:2

Journaling

ꕤ Praise Reports ꕤ ꕤPrayer Requests ꕤ

Great is our Lord and abundant in strength; His understanding is infinite. Psalm 147:5

Journaling

ꕤ Praise Reports ꕤ ꕤPrayer Requests ꕤ

Gracious *is* the LORD, and righteous; Yes, our God *is* merciful. Psalm 116:5

Journaling

 Praise Reports Prayer Requests

I have set the LORD always before me; because *He is* at my right hand I shall not be moved. Psalm 16:8

Journaling

☙ Praise Reports ❧ ☙Prayer Requests ☙

You will show me the path of life; In Your presence *is* fullness of joy;
At Your right hand *are* pleasures forevermore. Psalm 16:11

Journaling

ꕤ Praise Reports ꕤ ꕤPrayer Requests ꕤ

Great is our Lord and abundant in strength; His understanding is infinite. Psalm 147:5

Journaling

ꕤ Praise Reports ꕤ ꕤPrayer Requests ꕤ

Show Your marvelous lovingkindness by Your right hand, O You who save those who trust *in You,* from those who rise up *against them.*
Keep me as the apple of Your eye; Hide me under the shadow of Your wings. Psalm 17:7, 8

Journaling

ꕤ Praise Reports ꕤ ꕤPrayer Requests ꕤ

I will love You, O LORD, my strength.
The LORD is my rock and my fortress and my deliverer…Psalm 18:1, 2a

Journaling

ᘓ Praise Reports ᘐ ᘓPrayer Requests ᘓ

My God, my strength, in whom I will trust;
My shield and the horn of my salvation, my stronghold. Psalm 18:2

Journaling

ꟹ Praise Reports ꟹ ꟹPrayer Requests ꟹ

I will call upon the LORD, *who is worthy* to be praised;
So shall I be saved from my enemies. Psalm 18:3

Journaling

ꟼ Praise Reports ꝏ ꟼPrayer Requests ꟼ

The law of the LORD *is* perfect, converting the soul;
The testimony of the LORD *is* sure, making wise the simple Psalm 19:7

Journaling

ꕥ Praise Reports ꕥ ꕥPrayer Requests ꕥ

Let the words of my mouth and the meditation of my heart
Be acceptable in Your sight, O LORD, my strength and my Redeemer. Psalm 19:14

Journaling

ꕥ Praise Reports ꕥ ꕥPrayer Requests ꕥ

The statutes of the LORD *are* right, rejoicing the heart;
The commandment of the LORD *is* pure, enlightening the eyes… Psalm 19:8

ꕤ Praise Reports ꕤ ꕤPrayer Requests ꕤ

The fear of the LORD *is* clean, enduring forever;
The judgments of the LORD *are* true *and* righteous altogether. Psalm 19:9

Journaling

༄ Praise Reports ༄ ༄Prayer Requests ༄

Let the words of my mouth and the meditation of my heart
Be acceptable in Your sight, O LORD, my strength and my Redeemer. Psalm 19:14

Journaling

ꝏ Praise Reports ꝏ ꝏPrayer Requests ꝏ

May the LORD answer you in the day of trouble; may the name of the God of Jacob defend you;
May He send you help from the sanctuary, and strengthen you out of Zion…Psalm 20:1-2

Journaling

ꟃ Praise Reports ꟃ ꟃPrayer Requests ꟃ

May He remember all your offerings,
And accept your burnt sacrifice. Selah Psalm 20:3

ꕥ Praise Reports ꕥ ꕥPrayer Requests ꕥ

Now I know that the LORD saves His anointed; He will answer him from His holy heaven
With the saving strength of His right hand. Psalm 20:6

Journaling

ꕤ Praise Reports ꕤ ꕤPrayer Requests ꕤ

Some *trust* in chariots, and some in horses;
But we will remember the name of the LORD our God. Psalm 20:7

Journaling

ꝏ Praise Reports ꝏ ꝏPrayer Requests ꝏ

The king shall have joy in Your strength, O LORD;
and in Your salvation how greatly shall he rejoice! Psalm 21:1

Journaling

ℵ Praise Reports ℵ ℵPrayer Requests ℵ

You have given him his heart's desire,
and have not withheld the request of his lips. Selah Psalm 21: 2

Journaling

ᘐ Praise Reports ᘓ ᘐPrayer Requests ᘐ

Be exalted, O LORD, in Your own strength!
We will sing and praise Your power. Psalm 21:13

Journaling

ࠀ Praise Reports ௸ ࠀPrayer Requests ࠀ

The LORD *is* my shepherd; I shall not want.
He makes me to lie down in green pastures; He leads me beside the still waters Psalm 23:1, 2

Journaling

ꕥ Praise Reports ꕤ ꕥPrayer Requests ꕥ

A posterity shall serve Him. It will be recounted of the Lord to the *next* generation,
They will come and declare His righteousness to a people who will be born,
That He has done *this.* *Psalm 22:30, 31*

Journaling

ꕤ Praise Reports ꕤ ꕤPrayer Requests ꕤ

He restores my soul; He leads me in the paths of righteousness
For His name's sake. Psalm 23:3

ꕥ Praise Reports ꕥ ꕥPrayer Requests ꕥ

All the ends of the world shall remember and turn to the LORD, and all the families of the nations shall worship before You. For the kingdom *is* the LORD's, and He rules over the nations.
Psalm 22:27, 28

Journaling

ꕥ Praise Reports ꕥ ꕥPrayer Requests ꕥ

Yea, though I walk through the valley of the shadow of death, I will fear no evil;
For You *are* with me; Your rod and Your staff, they comfort me. Psalm 23:4

Journaling

ꕤ Praise Reports ꕤ ꕤPrayer Requests ꕤ

Surely goodness and mercy shall follow me All the days of my life;
And I will dwell in the house of the LORD Forever. Psalm 23:6

Journaling

ꕤ Praise Reports ꕤ ꕤPrayer Requests ꕤ

Who may ascend into the hill of the LORD? Or who may stand in His holy place?
He who has clean hands and a pure heart, Who has not lifted up his soul to an idol,
Nor sworn deceitfully. He shall receive blessing from the LORD, And righteousness from the
God of his salvation. This *is* Jacob, the generation of those who seek Him, who seek Your face.
Selah Psalm 24:3-6

Journaling

ꟸ Praise Reports ꟷ ꟸPrayer Requests ꟸ

The earth *is* the LORD's, and all its fullness,
The world and those who dwell therein. Psalm 24:1

Journaling

ꕤ Praise Reports ꕤ ꕤPrayer Requests ꕤ

O LORD, You have searched me and known *me.* You know my sitting down and my rising up; You understand my thought afar off. Psalm 139:1, 2

Journaling

ꟹ Praise Reports ꟹ ꟹPrayer Requests ꟹ

Where can I go from Your Spirit? Or where can I flee from Your presence?
If I ascend into heaven, You *are* there; If I make my bed in hell, behold, You *are there.*
Psalm 139:7, 8

Journaling

ঌ Praise Reports ০ ঌPrayer Requests ঌ

If I take the wings of the morning, and dwell in the uttermost parts of the sea,
Even there Your hand shall lead me, and Your right hand shall hold me. Psalm 139:9, 10

Journaling

ꕥ Praise Reports ꕥ ꕥPrayer Requests ꕥ

Lift up your heads, O you gates! and be lifted up, you everlasting doors!
And the King of glory shall come in. Psalm 24:7

Journaling

꧁ Praise Reports ꧂ ꧁Prayer Requests ꧂

Who *is* this King of glory? The LORD strong and mighty,
The LORD mighty in battle. Psalm 24:8

ꕥ Praise Reports ꕥ ꕥPrayer Requests ꕥ

Show me Your ways, O LORD; Teach me Your paths.
Lead me in Your truth and teach me, For You *are* the God of my salvation;
On You I wait all the day. Psalm 25:4, 5

Journaling

ꕤ Praise Reports ꕤ ꕤPrayer Requests ꕤ

The LORD *is* my light and my salvation; Whom shall I fear?
The LORD *is* the strength of my life; Of whom shall I be afraid? Psalm 27:1, 2

Journaling

ꕤ Praise Reports ꕤ ꕤPrayer Requests ꕤ

Though an army may encamp against me, my heart shall not fear;
Though war may rise against me, in this I *will be* confident. Psalm 27:3

Journaling

ꕥ Praise Reports ꕥ ꕥPrayer Requests ꕥ

One *thing* I have desired of the LORD, That will I seek:
That I may dwell in the house of the LORD All the days of my life,
To behold the beauty of the LORD, and to inquire in His temple. Psalm 27:4

ꕤ Praise Reports ꕤ ꕤPrayer Requests ꕤ

Good and upright *is* the LORD; Therefore He teaches sinners in the way.
The humble He guides in justice, and the humble He teaches His way. Psalm 25:8, 9

Journaling

ꕥ Praise Reports ꕥ ꕥPrayer Requests ꕥ

Who *is* the man that fears the LORD? Him shall He teach in the way He chooses.
He himself shall dwell in prosperity, And his descendants shall inherit the earth. Psalm 25:12, 13

Journaling

ꟹ Praise Reports ꟹ ꟹPrayer Requests ꟹ

The counsel of the Lord stands forever, The plans of His heart to all generations. Psalm 33:11

Journaling

ฆ Praise Reports ꕤ ฆPrayer Requests ฆ

Teach me Your way, O LORD,
And lead me in a smooth path, because of my enemies. Psalm 27:11

Journaling

༄ Praise Reports ༄ ༄Prayer Requests ༄

You will guide me with Your counsel, And afterward receive me *to* glory. Psalm 73:24

Journaling

ꕥ Praise Reports ꕥ ꕥPrayer Requests ꕥ

Examine me, O LORD, and prove me;
Try my mind and my heart. Psalm 26:1, 2

Journaling

ꟸ Praise Reports ꟹ ꟸPrayer Requests ꟸ

Your testimonies also *are* my delight *And* my counselors. Psalm 119:24

Journaling

ꕥ Praise Reports ꕥ ꕥPrayer Requests ꕥ

May He grant you according to your heart's *desire and* fulfill all your purpose. Psalm 20:4

Journaling

ꕤ Praise Reports ꕤ ꕤPrayer Requests ꕤ

Gird Your sword upon *Your* thigh, O Mighty One,
With Your glory and Your majesty. Psalm 45:3

Journaling

ꕥ Praise Reports ꕤ ꕥPrayer Requests ꕥ

Your throne, O God, *is* forever and ever;
A scepter of righteousness *is* the scepter of Your kingdom. Psalm 45:6

Journaling

ꝏ Praise Reports ꝏ ꝏPrayer Requests ꝏ

God *is* our refuge and strength, A very present help in trouble.
Therefore we will not fear, even though the earth be removed… Psalm 46:1, 2

Journaling

ꕤ Praise Reports ꕤ ꕤPrayer Requests ꕤ

For the LORD Most High *is* awesome;
He is a great King over all the earth. Psalm 47:2

ꕥ Praise Reports ꕥ ꕥPrayer Requests ꕥ

God reigns over the nations; God sits on His holy throne.
The princes of the people have gathered together, the people of the God of Abraham.
For the shields of the earth *belong* to God; He is greatly exalted. Psalm 47:8, 9

Journaling

꧁ Praise Reports ꧂ ꧁Prayer Requests ꧂

The Mighty One, God the LORD, has spoken and called the earth
From the rising of the sun to its going down. Psalm 50:1

Journaling

༄ Praise Reports ༄ ༄Prayer Requests ༄

Whoever offers praise glorifies Me; and to him who orders *his* conduct *aright*
I will show the salvation of God. Psalm 50:23

Journaling

ꕤ Praise Reports ꕤ ꕤPrayer Requests ꕤ

Call upon Me in the day of trouble;
I will deliver you, and you shall glorify Me. Psalm 50:15

Journaling

ꕤ Praise Reports ꕤ ꕤPrayer Requests ꕤ

Great *is* the LORD, and greatly to be praised in the city of our God,
In His holy mountain. Psalm 48:1

Journaling

❧ Praise Reports ☙ ❧Prayer Requests ❧

Before the mountains were brought forth, Or ever You had formed the earth and the world, Even from everlasting to everlasting, You *are* God. Psalm 90:2

Journaling

ᘓ Praise Reports ᘐ ᘓPrayer Requests ᘓ

For the Lord *is* good; His mercy *is* everlasting, And His truth *endures* to all generations.
Psalm 100:5

Journaling

ꕤ Praise Reports ꕤ ꕤPrayer Requests ꕤ

Surely he will never be shaken; The righteous will be in everlasting remembrance. Psalm 112:6

Journaling

ꕥ Praise Reports ꕥ ꕥPrayer Requests ꕥ

Your kingdom *is* an everlasting kingdom, and
Your dominion *endures* throughout all generations. Psalm 145:13

Journaling

ꕥ Praise Reports ꕥ ꕥPrayer Requests ꕥ

The Lord will give strength to His people;
The Lord will bless His people with peace. Psalm 29:11

Journaling

ꕥ Praise Reports ꕥ ꕥPrayer Requests ꕥ

...the meek shall inherit the earth,
And shall delight themselves in the abundance of peace. Psalm 37:11

Journaling

ꟸ Praise Reports ꟹ ꟸPrayer Requests ꟸ

Mark the blameless *man and* observe the upright; For the future of *that* man *is* peace.
Psalm 37:37

Journaling

ꕥ Praise Reports ꕥ ꕥPrayer Requests ꕥ

A father of the fatherless, a defender of widows, *Is* God in His holy habitation. Psalm 78:5

Journaling

ꕥ Praise Reports ꕥ ꕥPrayer Requests ꕥ

For you created my inmost being; you knit me together in my mother's womb.
I praise you because I am fearfully and wonderfully made;
your works are wonderful, I know that full well. Psalm 139:13, 14

Journaling

ᘐ Praise Reports ᘓ ᘐPrayer Requests ᘐ

Search me, God, and know my heart; test me and know my anxious thoughts.
See if there is any offensive way in me and lead me in the way everlasting. Psalm 139:23, 24

Journaling

ꕥ Praise Reports ꕥ ꕥPrayer Requests ꕥ

We will not hide *them* from their children, telling the generation to come the praises of the Lord, And His strength and His wonderful works that He has done. Psalm 78:4

Journaling

ꕤ Praise Reports ꕤ ꕤPrayer Requests ꕤ

That the generation to come might know *them,* The children *who* would be born, *That* they may arise and declare *them* to their children. Psalm 78:6

Journaling

ꕥ Praise Reports ꕥ ꕥPrayer Requests ꕥ

… the mercy of the LORD *is* from everlasting to everlasting on those who fear Him,
And His righteousness to children's children, To such as keep His covenant,
And to those who remember His commandments to do them. Psalm 103:17, 18

ꕥ Weekly Prayer Requests ꕥ

Now to him who is able to do immeasurably more than all we ask or imagine, according to his power that is at work within us, to him be glory in the church and in Christ Jesus throughout all generations, forever and ever! Amen.
Eph. 3:20, 21 NIV

Therefore I exhort first of all that supplications, prayers, intercessions, *and* giving of thanks be made for all men, for kings and all who are in authority, that we may lead a quiet and peaceable life in all godliness and reverence. For this *is* good and acceptable in the sight of God our Savior… 1 Timothy 2:1-3

Family ______________________________

____

____

Church ______________________________

____

____

Missionaries ______________________________

____

____

Government ______________________________

____

____

Workplaces ______________________________

____

____

Military ______________________________

____

____

School ______________________________

____

____

Other ______________________________

____

____

Women of Destiny

Call to Me, and I will answer you, and show you great and mighty things, which you do not know.' Jeremiah 33:3

Family ______________________________

____

____

Church ______________________________

____

____

Missionaries ______________________________

____

____

Government ______________________________

____

____

Workplaces ______________________________

____

____

Military ______________________________

____

____

School ______________________________

____

____

Other ______________________________

____

____

Therefore I exhort first of all that supplications, prayers, intercessions, *and* giving of thanks be made for all men, for kings and all who are in authority, that we may lead a quiet and peaceable life in all godliness and reverence. For this *is* good and acceptable in the sight of God our Savior… 1 Timothy 2:1-3

Family ______________________________

____

____

Church ______________________________

____

____

Missionaries ______________________________

____

____

Government ______________________________

____

____

Workplaces ______________________________

____

____

Military ______________________________

____

____

School ______________________________

____

____

Other ______________________________

____

____

Women of Destiny

Call to Me, and I will answer you, and show you great and mighty things, which you do not know.' Jeremiah 33:3

Family ______________________________

____

____

Church ______________________________

____

____

Missionaries ______________________________

____

____

Government ______________________________

____

____

Workplaces ______________________________

____

____

Military ______________________________

____

____

School ______________________________

____

____

Other ______________________________

____

____

Women of Destiny

Therefore I exhort first of all that supplications, prayers, intercessions, *and* giving of thanks be made for all men, for kings and all who are in authority, that we may lead a quiet and peaceable life in all godliness and reverence. For this *is* good and acceptable in the sight of God our Savior... 1 Timothy 2:1-3

Family ____

____

____

Church ____

____

____

Missionaries ____

____

____

Government ____

____

____

Workplaces ____

____

____

Military ____

____

____

School ____

____

____

Other ____

____

____

Women of Destiny

Call to Me, and I will answer you, and show you great and mighty things, which you do not know.' Jeremiah 33:3

Family ______________________________

____

____

Church ______________________________

____

____

Missionaries ______________________________

____

____

Government ______________________________

____

____

Workplaces ______________________________

____

____

Military ______________________________

____

____

School ______________________________

____

____

Other ______________________________

____

____

Therefore I exhort first of all that supplications, prayers, intercessions, *and* giving of thanks be made for all men, for kings and all who are in authority, that we may lead a quiet and peaceable life in all godliness and reverence. For this *is* good and acceptable in the sight of God our Savior… 1 Timothy 2:1-3

Family ______________________________

____

____

Church ______________________________

____

____

Missionaries ______________________________

____

____

Government ______________________________

____

____

Workplaces ______________________________

____

____

Military ______________________________

____

____

School ______________________________

____

____

Other ______________________________

____

____

Women of Destiny

Call to Me, and I will answer you, and show you great and mighty things, which you do not know.' Jeremiah 33:3

Family ____

____

____

Church ____

____

____

Missionaries ____

____

____

Government ____

____

____

Workplaces ____

____

____

Military ____

____

____

School ____

____

____

Other ____

____

____

Therefore I exhort first of all that supplications, prayers, intercessions, *and* giving of thanks be made for all men, for kings and all who are in authority, that we may lead a quiet and peaceable life in all godliness and reverence. For this *is* good and acceptable in the sight of God our Savior… 1 Timothy 2:1-3

Family ____

____

____

Church ____

____

____

Missionaries ____

____

____

Government ____

____

____

Workplaces ____

____

____

Military ____

____

____

School ____

____

____

Other ____

____

____

Women of Destiny

Call to Me, and I will answer you, and show you great and mighty things, which you do not know.' Jeremiah 33:3

Family ____

____

____

Church ____

____

____

Missionaries ____

____

____

Government ____

____

____

Workplaces ____

____

____

Military ____

____

____

School ____

____

____

Other ____

____

____

Women of Destiny

Therefore I exhort first of all that supplications, prayers, intercessions, *and* giving of thanks be made for all men, for kings and all who are in authority, that we may lead a quiet and peaceable life in all godliness and reverence. For this *is* good and acceptable in the sight of God our Savior... 1 Timothy 2:1-3

Family ______________________________

____

____

Church ______________________________

____

____

Missionaries ______________________________

____

____

Government ______________________________

____

____

Workplaces ______________________________

____

____

Military ______________________________

____

____

School ______________________________

____

____

Other ______________________________

____

____

Women of Destiny

Call to Me, and I will answer you, and show you great and mighty things, which you do not know.' Jeremiah 33:3

Family ____

____

____

Church ____

____

____

Missionaries ____

____

____

Government ____

____

____

Workplaces ____

____

____

Military ____

____

____

School ____

____

____

Other ____

____

____

Therefore I exhort first of all that supplications, prayers, intercessions, *and* giving of thanks be made for all men, for kings and all who are in authority, that we may lead a quiet and peaceable life in all godliness and reverence. For this *is* good and acceptable in the sight of God our Savior... 1 Timothy 2:1-3

Family ____

____

____

Church ____

____

____

Missionaries ____

____

____

Government ____

____

____

Workplaces ____

____

____

Military ____

____

____

School ____

____

____

Other ____

____

____

Women of Destiny

Call to Me, and I will answer you, and show you great and mighty things, which you do not know.' Jeremiah 33:3

Family ____________________

____

____

Church ____________________

____

____

Missionaries ____________________

____

____

Government ____________________

____

____

Workplaces ____________________

____

____

Military ____________________

____

____

School ____________________

____

____

Other ____________________

____

____

Women of Destiny

Therefore I exhort first of all that supplications, prayers, intercessions, *and* giving of thanks be made for all men, for kings and all who are in authority, that we may lead a quiet and peaceable life in all godliness and reverence. For this *is* good and acceptable in the sight of God our Savior… 1 Timothy 2:1-3

Family ____

____

____

Church ____

____

____

Missionaries ____

____

____

Government ____

____

____

Workplaces ____

____

____

Military ____

____

____

School ____

____

____

Other ____

____

____

Women of Destiny

Call to Me, and I will answer you, and show you great and mighty things, which you do not know.' Jeremiah 33:3

Family ______________________________

____

____

Church ______________________________

____

____

Missionaries ______________________________

____

____

Government ______________________________

____

____

Workplaces ______________________________

____

____

Military ______________________________

____

____

School ______________________________

____

____

Other ______________________________

____

____

Therefore I exhort first of all that supplications, prayers, intercessions, *and* giving of thanks be made for all men, for kings and all who are in authority, that we may lead a quiet and peaceable life in all godliness and reverence. For this *is* good and acceptable in the sight of God our Savior… 1 Timothy 2:1-3

Family ____

____

____

Church ____

____

____

Missionaries ____

____

____

Government ____

____

____

Workplaces ____

____

____

Military ____

____

____

School ____

____

____

Other ____

____

____

Women of Destiny

Call to Me, and I will answer you, and show you great and mighty things, which you do not know.' Jeremiah 33:3

Family ____

____

____

Church ____

____

____

Missionaries ____

____

____

Government ____

____

____

Workplaces ____

____

____

Military ____

____

____

School ____

____

____

Other ____

____

____

Therefore I exhort first of all that supplications, prayers, intercessions, *and* giving of thanks be made for all men, for kings and all who are in authority, that we may lead a quiet and peaceable life in all godliness and reverence. For this *is* good and acceptable in the sight of God our Savior... 1 Timothy 2:1-3

Family ____________________

____

____

Church ____________________

____

____

Missionaries ____________________

____

____

Government ____________________

____

____

Workplaces ____________________

____

____

Military ____________________

____

____

School ____________________

____

____

Other ____________________

____

____

Women of Destiny

Call to Me, and I will answer you, and show you great and mighty things, which you do not know.' Jeremiah 33:3

Family ____

____

____

Church ____

____

____

Missionaries ____

____

____

Government ____

____

____

Workplaces ____

____

____

Military ____

____

____

School ____

____

____

Other ____

____

____

Women of Destiny

Therefore I exhort first of all that supplications, prayers, intercessions, *and* giving of thanks be made for all men, for kings and all who are in authority, that we may lead a quiet and peaceable life in all godliness and reverence. For this *is* good and acceptable in the sight of God our Savior… 1 Timothy 2:1-3

Family ____________________

____

____

Church ____________________

____

____

Missionaries ____________________

____

____

Government ____________________

____

____

Workplaces ____________________

____

____

Military ____________________

____

____

School ____________________

____

____

Other ____________________

____

____

Women of Destiny

Call to Me, and I will answer you, and show you great and mighty things, which you do not know.' Jeremiah 33:3

Family ______________________________

____

____

Church ______________________________

____

____

Missionaries ______________________________

____

____

Government ______________________________

____

____

Workplaces ______________________________

____

____

Military ______________________________

____

____

School ______________________________

____

____

Other ______________________________

____

____

Therefore I exhort first of all that supplications, prayers, intercessions, *and* giving of thanks be made for all men, for kings and all who are in authority, that we may lead a quiet and peaceable life in all godliness and reverence. For this *is* good and acceptable in the sight of God our Savior… 1 Timothy 2:1-3

Family ______________________________

____

____

Church ______________________________

____

____

Missionaries ______________________________

____

____

Government ______________________________

____

____

Workplaces ______________________________

____

____

Military ______________________________

____

____

School ______________________________

____

____

Other ______________________________

____

____

Women of Destiny

Call to Me, and I will answer you, and show you great and mighty things, which you do not know.' Jeremiah 33:3

Family ______________________________

____

____

Church ______________________________

____

____

Missionaries ______________________________

____

____

Government ______________________________

____

____

Workplaces ______________________________

____

____

Military ______________________________

____

____

School ______________________________

____

____

Other ______________________________

____

____

Therefore I exhort first of all that supplications, prayers, intercessions, *and* giving of thanks be made for all men, for kings and all who are in authority, that we may lead a quiet and peaceable life in all godliness and reverence. For this *is* good and acceptable in the sight of God our Savior... 1 Timothy 2:1-3

Family ____

____

____

Church ____

____

____

Missionaries ____

____

____

Government ____

____

____

Workplaces ____

____

____

Military ____

____

____

School ____

____

____

Other ____

____

____

Women of Destiny

Call to Me, and I will answer you, and show you great and mighty things, which you do not know.' Jeremiah 33:3

Family ______________________________

____

____

Church ______________________________

____

____

Missionaries ______________________________

____

____

Government ______________________________

____

____

Workplaces ______________________________

____

____

Military ______________________________

____

____

School ______________________________

____

____

Other ______________________________

____

____

Therefore I exhort first of all that supplications, prayers, intercessions, *and* giving of thanks be made for all men, for kings and all who are in authority, that we may lead a quiet and peaceable life in all godliness and reverence. For this *is* good and acceptable in the sight of God our Savior… 1 Timothy 2:1-3

Family ____

____

____

Church ____

____

____

Missionaries ____

____

____

Government ____

____

____

Workplaces ____

____

____

Military ____

____

____

School ____

____

____

Other ____

____

____

Women of Destiny

Call to Me, and I will answer you, and show you great and mighty things, which you do not know.' Jeremiah 33:3

Family ______________________________

____

____

Church ______________________________

____

____

Missionaries ______________________________

____

____

Government ______________________________

____

____

Workplaces ______________________________

____

____

Military ______________________________

____

____

School ______________________________

____

____

Other ______________________________

____

____

Women of Destiny

Therefore I exhort first of all that supplications, prayers, intercessions, *and* giving of thanks be made for all men, for kings and all who are in authority, that we may lead a quiet and peaceable life in all godliness and reverence. For this *is* good and acceptable in the sight of God our Savior... 1 Timothy 2:1-3

Family ______________________________

____

____

Church ______________________________

____

____

Missionaries ______________________________

____

____

Government ______________________________

____

____

Workplaces ______________________________

____

____

Military ______________________________

____

____

School ______________________________

____

____

Other ______________________________

____

____

Women of Destiny

Call to Me, and I will answer you, and show you great and mighty things, which you do not know.' Jeremiah 33:3

Family ____

____

____

Church ____

____

____

Missionaries ____

____

____

Government ____

____

____

Workplaces ____

____

____

Military ____

____

____

School ____

____

____

Other ____

____

____

Therefore I exhort first of all that supplications, prayers, intercessions, *and* giving of thanks be made for all men, for kings and all who are in authority, that we may lead a quiet and peaceable life in all godliness and reverence. For this *is* good and acceptable in the sight of God our Savior… 1 Timothy 2:1-3

Family ____

____

____

Church ____

____

____

Missionaries ____

____

____

Government ____

____

____

Workplaces ____

____

____

Military ____

____

____

School ____

____

____

Other ____

____

____

Women of Destiny

Call to Me, and I will answer you, and show you great and mighty things, which you do not know.' Jeremiah 33:3

Family ____

____

____

Church ____

____

____

Missionaries ____________________________________

____

____

Government ____________________________________

____

____

Workplaces ____________________________________

____

____

Military ____

____

____

School ____

____

____

Other ____

____

____

Women of Destiny

Therefore I exhort first of all that supplications, prayers, intercessions, *and* giving of thanks be made for all men, for kings and all who are in authority, that we may lead a quiet and peaceable life in all godliness and reverence. For this *is* good and acceptable in the sight of God our Savior... 1 Timothy 2:1-3

Family ____

____

____

Church ____

____

____

Missionaries ____

____

____

Government ____

____

____

Workplaces ____

____

____

Military ____

____

____

School ____

____

____

Other ____

____

____

Women of Destiny

Call to Me, and I will answer you, and show you great and mighty things, which you do not know.' Jeremiah 33:3

Family

Church

Missionaries

Government

Workplaces

Military

School

Other

Women of Destiny

Therefore I exhort first of all that supplications, prayers, intercessions, *and* giving of thanks be made for all men, for kings and all who are in authority, that we may lead a quiet and peaceable life in all godliness and reverence. For this *is* good and acceptable in the sight of God our Savior... 1 Timothy 2:1-3

Family ______________________________

____

____

Church ______________________________

____

____

Missionaries ______________________________

____

____

Government ______________________________

____

____

Workplaces ______________________________

____

____

Military ______________________________

____

____

School ______________________________

____

____

Other ______________________________

____

____

꧁ Prayer Resources ꧂

"Again I say to you that if two of you agree on earth concerning anything that they ask, it will be done for them by My Father in heaven. For where two or three are gathered together in My name, I am there in the midst of them." Matthew 18:19-20

Every Home for Christ Prayer Maps www.ehc.org/resources

Intercessors for America Prayer Calendars www.ifapray.org

International House of Prayer Streaming 24/7 Prayer www.ihopkc.org

Lydia Fellowship International www.lydiafellowship.org

Moms in Prayer International Prayer Sheets Character, Attributes, and Names of God www.momsinprayer.org

National Day of Prayer www.nationaldayofprayer.org

Operation World Prayer Guide www.operationworld.org

Power of A Praying Woman www.stormieomartian.com/prayercommunity

Prayer cast www.prayercast.com

Prayers that Avail Much www.prayers.org

Blessed is the man that walks not in the counsel of the ungodly, nor stands in the
way of sinners, nor sits in the seat of the scornful. But his delight is in the law of the LORD;
and in his law does he meditate day and night. And he shall be like a tree
planted by the rivers of water, that brings forth its fruit in its season; his leaf also shall not wither;
and whatsoever he does shall prosper. Psalm 1:1-3

ꕤ Prayers for Salvation and Deliverance ꕤ

Open _______'s eyes and turn him/her from darkness to light, and from the power of Satan to God, so that he/she may receive forgiveness of sins and a place among those who are sanctified by faith in Jesus. From Acts 26:18

May…the eyes of your understanding being enlightened; that you may know what is the hope of His calling, what are the riches of the glory of His inheritance in the saints… Ephesians 1:18

ꕥEpilogueꕥ

Remember the former things of old, For I *am* God, and *there is* no other;
I am God, and *there is* none like Me, Declaring the end from the beginning,
And from ancient times *things* that are not *yet* done, Saying, 'My counsel shall stand,
And I will do all My pleasure,' Isaiah 46:9, 10

In the beginning God created the heavens and the earth. Then God said, "Let Us make man in Our image, according to Our likeness; let them have dominion over the fish of the sea, over the birds of the air, and over the cattle, over all the earth and over every creeping thing that creeps on the earth." So God created man in His *own* image; in the image of God He created him; male and female He created them. Then God blessed them, and God said to them, "Be fruitful and multiply; fill the earth and subdue it; have dominion over the fish of the sea, over the birds of the air, and over every living thing that moves on the earth." Genesis 1:1, 26-29

In the beginning was the Word, and the Word was with God, and the Word was God. He was in the beginning with God. All things were made through Him, and without Him nothing was made that was made. In Him was life, and the life was the light of men. And the light shines in the darkness, and the darkness did not comprehend it. John 1:1

The Bible is one book of 66 smaller books and the first part of the book (the Old Testament) sets the stage, introduces the characters, lays down the Law and provides the reasoning behind God's judgment – and His deliverance – at the very end of the book. It's common for readers of the book of Revelation to ignore the cross references and not look at the context of the Old Testament passages that are quoted throughout Revelation. But there is a reason Revelation is filled with quotes directing you to the beginning of the book – passages in Exodus, Deuteronomy, Isaiah, Jeremiah, Ezekiel, and Daniel, just to name a few.

Jesus, the Word of God was coexistent in the beginning with the Father. He was sent into the world to reveal the Father's heart. We were created in the Father's image as eternal beings with a triune nature. We are spirit, we have a soul (mind, will, and intellect), and we live in a body. The Father's desire is that every be reconciled to Him and walk in the authority relegated to mankind. We are called to dispel darkness with the light of redemption and salvation through Jesus' blood that was shed on Calvary.

There is a clear attack on the family and godly manhood and womanhood. It is vital that we help the next generation to understand that their identity begins with the Creator's mind and design. As we go forth as ambassadors representing the eternal Creator, it is essential that we see them in light of God's purpose for their lives. This can only happen as we seek Him first for guidance. If we are to be firmly rooted and lay a firm foundation for faith development, we must know God as Creator and realize that in His sovereignty He has a plan. As you meditate upon scripture, ask the following questions: *What does the text say? What does it mean, in light of who it was written to and the time at which it was written? What does this mean to me and how I should live? How does this biblical truth affect your motivation and the strategies implemented for making disciples?* May our eyes be opened to the True Light who desires to shine through us to transform our hearts, homes, schools, community, nation, and the world.

The Shepherd's Academy
❧School Year Calendar 2020-21☙

The Shepherd's Academy is an exemplary leadership preparatory pre-K-12th grade Christian school. We are committed to providing students with a high-quality Christ-centered education. Our mission is to partner with Christian families to assist in the training of their children to love, serve, and be conformed to the image of Jesus Christ: and at the same time offer a superior education. We provide young children with time to play, create and use their imaginations in a Christ-centered environment with Bible based curricula. Our staff integrates technology in order to promote the development of essential technical skills children need to thrive in the 21st century workforce.

March 27	Spring Break Camp Staff Orientation
March 30-31	Spring Break STREAM Camp
April 1-3	Spring Break STREAM Camp
May 21, 22	Camp Destiny Staff Orientation
May 26	Camp Destiny
July 24	Camp Destiny ends
July 27-	Staff Orientation
August 3	Placement Tests/Open House
July 29	Administrative Staff Meeting
July 31	Family Orientation
July 27-31	Pre-planning
August 2	Family Orientation
August 3	First Day of School
August 24	Lambs Parent Service Organization Officer's Meeting
September 7	Labor Day (School Closed)
September 7-11	International Missions Week
September 11	Christmas Card Sale Begins
September 15	Parent Teacher Fellowship Meeting
September 24	School Picture Day
October 1	Pizza Hut Book It! Program Begins
	Christmas Card Sale Ends-Proceeds Due
October 9	Early Release
	Staff Development
October 22-23	Staff Development (School Closed) ACSI PD Forum
October 20	Parent Teacher Fellowship Meeting
October 16	Progress Report
October 22	Parent Teacher Conference Night
November 1	Christmas Banquet Ticket Sale Begins
November 9	Lambs Parent Service Organization Officer's Meeting
November 20	Nursing Home – Dress Rehearsal
November 24	Christian Heritage Assembly Program
	Staff meeting
November 25-27	Thanksgiving Break (School Closed)
December 13	Annual Lamb of God Christmas Banquet
December 18	End of First Semester-Report Card
December 21-January 1	Christmas Break (School Closed)
January 4-5	Staff Development (School Closed)
	Open enrollment-Benefits meetings

Women of Destiny

	New Family Orientation
January 7	School Picture (Make-up day)
January 18	M. L. King Jr. Day – Community Service Day (School Closed)
January 19	Parent Teacher Fellowship Meeting
February 14	Valentine's Day-Ash Wednesday Chapel Program
February 15	Free Indeed Presentations (early release)
February 17	President's Day (School Closed)
	Staff meeting Teacher Planning ½ day
February 18	Career Day
February 16	Parent Teacher Fellowship Meeting
March 2	Six Flags Read to Succeed Deadline
March 5	Basketball Banquet
March 12	Student Holiday/Professional Development
March 16	Spring Festival and Parent Teacher Fellowship Meeting
March 19	Progress Report
March 22-26	Atlanta Science Festival Field Trips TBD
April 5-9	Spring Break
	Fine Arts and Sports – Camp Destiny
April 2	Good Friday (School Closed)
April 16	Cap & gown yearbook order deadline
April 19-23	Standardized Testing
April 23	Parent Teacher Conference Night
April 26	Lambs Parent Service Organization Officer's Meeting
May 3-7	Teacher Appreciation Week
May 6	National Day of Prayer
	State Capitol Tour
May 6	Field Day/May Day Events
May 7	Moms-Dads Day Sale
May 7	Mother's Luncheon
May 7	National Teacher Appreciation Day - Early Release
May 21	Graduation Ceremony & Honor's Assembly
	Last Day of School - Report Cards
May 24	Teacher Post Planning (School Closed)
May 27-28	Camp Destiny Staff Orientation
May 31	Memorial Day (School Closed)
June 1	Camp Destiny Summer Enrichment Program Begins

Moms in Prayer meeting Tuesdays 5-6 p.m.
Father's Night Out meets the 3rd Friday of each month 5-7 p.m.
Molding Mighty Men-Boys mentoring program meets 1st Saturday of the month
Effective parenting classes are held Wednesday 6-7:30 p.m. during the first semester
Crown financial bible study classes are held Wednesday 6-7:30 p.m. during the second semester
Administrative Staff Meetings are held Wednesdays 1:30-2:30 p.m.
Infant and Toddler Team meetings are held Thursdays 1:30-2:30 p.m.
Preschool Staff meetings are held the first Thursday of each month 1:30-2:30 p.m.
Professional Learning Community meetings dates and times are TBD
Unite! Marriage Conference for Couples dates and times are TBD

This calendar includes 180 student Pre-K-12th gr. contact days, ten professional development days for staff members. Child care services are typically available for pre-registered students as posted in the office. Dates are subject to change.

Women of Destiny

The Shepherd's Academy for Teaching Excellence

☙Academic Calendar❧

The Shepherd's Academy for Teaching Excellence is a vocational training program that equips ministers and serves early childhood educators and program administrators. We are an education consulting firm specializing in professional development for early childhood education organizations. We provide inspirational staff development and business consulting for administrators and teachers of programs for young children. Our objectives are to ensure optimal development of children by developing programs that engage every learner and to improve processes and performance in order to provide the best service possible to young children.

The Shepherd's Academy for Teaching Excellence provides many Georgia Department of Early Care and Learning: Bright from the Start, Council for Professional Recognition, and Georgia Department of Education Office of Professional Learning courses. All policies and procedures are in compliance with the National Health and Safety Standards established by the American Academy of Pediatrics, the National Board of Health, National Association for the Education of Young Children (NAEYC), the Association of Christian Schools International, and the Southern Association of Colleges and Schools Commission on Colleges accreditation (Advanced ED Georgia) standards for quality schools; and federal, state, and local regulations. We are a 501(c)3 corporation that is organized for charitable, religious, educational, and scientific purposes. Our primary goal is to equip kingdom educators to impact the world for Christ.

The Shepherd's Academy for Teaching Excellence uses a standard academic year as defined by a fall, spring and summer semester. Fall and spring semesters last for eighteen weeks. Summer semester lasts eight weeks. The academic calendar provides necessary information to assist adult education students in developing their class schedules, including the official term start and end dates, registration deadlines, payment deadlines, add/drop dates and holiday breaks. Be sure to review your academic calendar prior to the start of each term.

...whatever you do, do it heartily, as to the Lord, and not to men Colossians 3:23

Fall 2020 Classes Begin	August 20, 2020
Labor Day - No Classes	September 7, 2020
Convocation - No Classes Between 3-5 P.M.	Traditionally Held In October On Friday Of Family Weekend
Veterans Day - No Classes	November 11, 2020
Thanksgiving Recess	November 23-27, 2020
Last Day Of Classes And Laboratory Sessions	December 4, 2020
Final Examinations	December 5, 2020
Winter 2020 Classes Begin	December 7, 2021

Christmas Holidays - No Classes	December 21- January 5, 2021
New Year's Holiday - No Classes	January 1, 2021
Spring 2020 Classes Begin	January 6, 2021
Martin Luther King Jr Holiday - No Classes	January 18, 2021
Spring Recess - No Classes	April 5-9, 2021
Last Day Of Classes And Laboratory Sessions	May 14, 2021
Final Examinations	May 15, 2021
Summer 2020 Classes Begin	June 7, 2021
Memorial Day Holiday -- No Classes	May 31, 2021
Last Day Of Classes And Laboratory Sessions	July 23, 2021

Go you therefore, and teach all nations, baptizing them in the name of the Father, and of the Son, and of the Holy Ghost: Teaching them to observe all things whatever I have commanded you: and, see, I am with you always, even to the end of the world. Amen. Matthew 28:19, 20

Women of Destiny

The Shepherd's Academy for Teaching Excellence

჻Course Descriptions჻

TSATE offers several courses that are approved by Georgia Department of Education: Office of Professional Learning; Georgia Department of Early Care ad Learning: Bright from the Start workshops; and the Council for Professional Recognition. It would be a delight to meet your adult vocational training and professional development needs. Many courses are offered online, onsite at your school, or face-to-face at our school. The course descriptions are indicated along with the Georgia Professional Development and Workforce Knowledge and Competencies below:

Administering and Planning Educational Programs for Young Children - (40 Hours face-to-face or online) * **4 PLUs**
This state credential for program directors covers the following topics: rules & regulations, legal issues, ethics, communication, child development, learning theories, strategic program planning, environmental rating scales, parent empowerment, anti-bias, professional development, accessing resources, staff selection and supervision, employment law and program/fiscal management (feasibility studies, budgeting, and funding). ADM 1-9

Brain Based Instruction in the Developmentally Appropriate Classroom **(4 hours face-to-face)**
A study of developmentally appropriate practices in the context of brain based teaching and learning for young children, birth through age 9. This workshop is an integrated curricular study of appropriate early childhood curriculum, materials, environments, assessments, expectations, instructional strategies, and considerations for early childhood educators. It is designed to enhance a participant's knowledge of brain research. Participants will explore ways to design brain-friendly and effective lesson plans using the latest scientific findings and discoveries. It prepares early educators by providing them with the essential elements needed to translate the biology of brain-based learning from theory into classroom practice. ECE 1.2, 1.3

Child Development Associate **(120 hours online or face-to-face)**
The CDA workshop prepares students for work in the early childhood care and education field. Courses are offered fully online and in a classroom format. Participants must be working with young children regularly either in a paid or volunteer position to fulfill their coursework requirements. It covers the growth and development of children birth to 5 years of age. The course is designed to be completed in 12 weeks; however, online candidates for the CDA may complete it in less time or take longer. The course is self-paced with a one year maximum completion time. ECE 1.1, 2.1, 3.2, 4.2, 5.1, 6.1

Classroom Management Strategy Toolbox - (4 hours face-to-face)
Participants explore the essential components of effective classroom management for the early childhood and elementary school-aged child (as defined by Robert Marzano). Teachers develop a menu of disciplinary interventions and strategies which include addressing personality and learning styles, developing age appropriate rules and procedures, and the importance of teacher-student relationships. This workshop provides early childhood educators with principles of child development and appropriate behavioral expectations. The importance of positive teacher/child interactions, planning developmentally appropriate learning experiences, guidance techniques, and the importance of supporting the family are emphasized. ECE 1.2, 5.3

***Every Child Learns Differently* -** (6 hours face-to-face)
This seminar equips early educators with differentiated instruction approaches to teaching and learning for preschool and primary students. Teachers learn to provide multiple options for taking in information and making sense of ideas.

Healthy and Safety Training and Orientation – (6 hours face-to-face or online)
Participants will gain a broad overview of the National Health and Safety Standards which promote the well being of children in educational environments (e.g. injury prevention strategies, exclusion guidelines for common childhood illnesses (i.e. asthma and allergies) and infectious diseases including MRSA and the H1N1 virus (swine flu), and guidelines for identifying risk factors and clues which indicate child maltreatment, prevention strategies and reporting procedures. ECE 1.4, 4.2, 6.1

Get Ready to Read! (2 hours face-to-face)
Learn about early literacy skills for young learners. Ensure that the three-five year olds in your care for are ready to read with this short, easy screening tool. Using developmental screenings to support development, growth, and learning. ECE 3.2 Goes perfectly with Reading is "Fun"damental workshop

Money, Money, Money [Basic Grant Writing for Educators] - (4 hours face-to-face or 8 hours online)
This workshop for both beginners and experienced grant writers helps them to develop ideas into winning proposals, target potential funders and understand the full proposal development, submission and review process. Participants should come with an idea for a grant proposal. By the end of the workshop, they will have an outline, resources necessary to expand the outline into a full proposal, strategies for finding funding and return to their schools with the knowledge and skills to receive the funds for organizational and community growth, vitality and sustainability. ECE 6.1, 6.3; ADM 2, 8

Professionalism (21st Century Parents and Teachers) - (4 hours face-to-face)
This workshop provides the early childhood educator with an understanding of the historical, philosophical, ethics and social foundations of the early childhood profession, and provides self-assessment opportunities, techniques which enhance family involvement and cultural sensitivity. Educators gain knowledge and skills to help problem solve and serve families in a professional manner. ECE 2.2, 6.1

Reading is "Fun"-damental (4 hours face-to-face)
Learn fun and effective ways to implement early literacy learning experiences based upon current research and developmentally appropriate practices for children birth through grade three. ECE 5.5, 5.6

The Way Kids Learn – (2 hours face-to-face)
Participants discover keys to cultivating optimal development by identifying the unique learning styles of children and environmental factors which influence learning. Explore developmentally appropriate learning experiences which engage every learner. Emphasis upon holistic development. ECE 5.4

Watch Me! Celebrating milestones and sharing concerns! (2 hours face-to-face)
Learn about developmental monitoring, the educator's role in monitoring, how to monitor development, and how to talk with families about their child's development. ECE 1.1, 1.2, 2.1, 2.3

Book Order Form

Title	Regular	Quantity	Subtotals
Classroom Management Strategy Toolbox: *Includes over 35 Proactive Strategies*	$10.00		
Classroom Management Strategy Toolbox Planner	$7.00		
Equipping and Empowering Early Educators	$20.00		
Early Education Program Administration Toolkit	$40.00		
Effective Planning and Administration of Early Education Programs	$50.00		
Exceptional Learners (Disorder) Fact Sheet Booklet	$10.00		
Firmly Rooted	$20.00		
He is…Planner and Journal for Christian Educators	$25.00		
Sets			
Classroom Management Strategy Toolbox & Planner	$15.00		
EE Program Administration Toolkit and Effective Planning and Administration Manual	$80.00		
EE Program Administration Toolkit, Effective Planning and Administration Manual, and Equipping & Empowering Early Educators	$100.00		
Bulk for staff development			
Classroom Management Strategy Toolbox *and the CMST Planner*	$100.00	10	
Equipping and Empowering Early Educators	$150.00	10	
Exceptional Learners Fact Sheet Booklet	$75.00	10	
Inspirational			
A Very Present Help for Women of Faith-*30 Day Devotional*	$10.00		
Ambassadors: Public Speaking for Christian Students	$15.00		
Bullies Don't Bother Me: *Biblical Conflict Resolution Strategies*	$10.00		
Christian Education Mandate	$10.00		
Women of Destiny Prayer Journal	$15.00		
Subtotal			
Standard shipping (8-10 business days) $4 first book, $1 each additional 1-$4, 2-$5, 3-$6, 4-$7, 5-$8, 6-$9, 7-$10, 8-$11, 9-$12, 10-$13, 11-$14, 12-$15			
Tax (Georgia residents only 6%) $5.00=$.30 $10.00=$.60 $15.00=$.90 $20.00=$1.20 $25.00=$1.50 $30.00=$1.80 $35.00=$2.10 $40.00=$2.40 $45.00-$2.70 $50.00=$3.00			
Total Due			

Order online at www.pennconsulting.org or www.amazon.com
Mail the order form to: Penn Consulting P. O. Box 392006 Snellville, GA 30039

Please make checks payable to: Penn Consulting

Book Order Form page 2

Ordered by Name	**Ship to** ordered by ___ same as
Business Name	**Business Name**
Address	
City State Zip	**Address**
Telephone	**Email**

Quantity	Item Description	Price Each	Subtotal
Subtotal			
Sales Tax GA Customers only add 6%			
Shipping (See chart on reverse)			
Total Due			

Payment Method

Check or money order enclosed or attached: Amount No.

Credit Card Authorization (Please print)

Cardholder name

Card number Exp. Date

CSC/CVV # Circle one: American Express MasterCard Visa

☐ Billing address, if different

Business Name

Billing/Shipping Address

City/State Zip

Made in the USA
Columbia, SC
24 December 2019

85754599R00102